DRIVE IT!

The Complete Book of

FORMULA FORD

Phillip Bingham

Foulis

Haynes

ISBN 0 85429 434 1

A FOULIS Motoring Book

Published by
Haynes Publishing Group
Sparkford, Yeovil, Somerset BA22 7JJ

Distributed in USA by:
Haynes Publications Inc.
861 Lawrence Drive, Newbury Park, California 91320 USA

Editor: Mansur Darlington
Layout design: Gill Carroll
Dust jacket design: Phill Jennings
Printed and bound by: J. H. Haynes & Co. Ltd.

Contents

Acknowledgements

The author sincerely hopes that this book will prove easier to read than it was to write. He also hopes that considerable gratitude may be accepted by contributors in lieu of payment or Pints. Such gratitude belongs to all those kind souls who moulded ideas so patiently, ran ghastly errands so willingly, and answered silly questions so sensibly.

Particular recognition is due to those who made direct editorial contributions: 1984 works Van Diemen driver, Mark Peters; *Motoring News* staff member, Simon Arron; designer and company director, Adrian Reynard; *Autosport* photographer, Jeff Bloxham; understated and underrated freelance cameraman, John Overton; and Haynes Publishing's red pen men, Rod Grainger and Mansur Darlington.

Other donations of time and effort were generously forthcoming from Tim Elkins, Calvin Fish, Joan and Roger Bingham, Mike O'Brien, Roy and Sally Fish, Val Adaway of Formula Services, Dennis Rushen and Robin Green, Ralph Firman, Ian Taylor, Richard Peacock, Graeme Glew, and last, but by no means least, the lovely lady who kept the whole project rolling, Linda McRae!

The Jim Russell International Racing Drivers School should not go without special thanks, partly for convincing the author of the tremendous value of such educational establishments, and largely for presenting him with the opportunity to experience Formula Ford racing from the cockpit. Thanks here to Mr Russell himself, scrupulous MD John Paine, erudite entertainer John Kirkpatrick, and Don, Fred, Colin, and Attleborough Audrey.

The circuit illustrations in Chapter Seven are the copyright of, and are reproduced by the kind permission of, the RAC Motor Sports Association.

Introduction

Formula Ford is motor racing's biggest success story. A story that started back in the optimistic days when, if the chart topping Beatles were to be believed, all you needed was love — and when, if the Managing Director of Motor Circuit Developments was to be believed, all you needed, all of a sudden, was a love of motor racing, and perhaps a little help from your friends, to become a *serious* racing driver. Like so many brave motor sport ideas since, Formula Ford was announced as an exciting new racing formula whose origins were wisely founded in the ceaseless search for close competition at low costs. *Un*like so many formulas introduced since, Formula Ford has not only survived, but thrived.

In the 17 years that this success story has enjoyed so far, much has changed. Motor racing's Eldorado for beginners is no different to any other: it has detractors who can argue, sometimes convincingly, that the gold has lost its glitter, or that greed has caused ruin. But happily it cannot be argued that the vital purpose of the formula has altered. Since that happy Sunday afternoon in July 1967, Formula Ford has always meant that 'serious' motor racing is no longer merely the preserve of the Idle Rich, but is realistically within the reach of all but the simply idle. It is not cheap, it is not easy, and it does not reward sheer natural driving ability alone, but it is still the most reliable means by which an aspiring professional racing driver can hope to illustrate his or her talent. Amateurism has been squeezed out, and professionalism and commercialism are the new prerequisites for success. Money talks louder than ever, and public personality can ultimately mean as much as driving prowess, but the essential attraction of Formula Ford — that it is Fair Play so far as the very nature of motor racing will allow — stays largely unchanged.

So do the pitfalls. The traps lying at every corner of every race, and every decision made every day between races, waiting to snare the unprepared or unwary. The many means by which talent can be swallowed without results, or effort obscured without reward; the many ways in which hard earnt racing budgets can be mis-spent, over-spent, and simply spent for nothing; the frequent instances when even the strongest motivation can be drained. Though Formula Ford's tremendous success is solidly founded on the possibility of the success it can bring to others, it also survives in spite of a-thousand-and-one miserable failures. Racing can be fun, but winning is deadly serious. For each of the few superstars it launches, Formula Ford may also destroy the morale, marriages, and mortgages of many. Whether it be through commitment without comprehension, optimism without reason, or effort without equipment, too many facts of racing life are learnt the 'hard way'.

This book will not turn you into the next World Champion, will not bring a queue of sponsors to your front door, but it might refresh the parts that other books cannot reach, and if it does go just a little way towards reducing the rigours of such common education by means of error, then it will have been amply justified. Certainly, if the unanimous opinions are to be accepted of those experts who live and breathe in the advancing industry called Formula Ford, such a book has been needed for a long time. Even experts have to learn the 'hard way'. Those who kindly assisted with the research of this work — the team managers, designers, manufacturers, drivers, sponsors, racing school tutors, and mechanics — never varied in their despondency. Each one is far too familiar with the pitfalls of Formula Ford: with naivety and novices. It is an unfortunate fact of life that the two words usually go together. And it is a sadder fact of motor racing life that lessons cannot only be hard, but also expensive.

No book in the world should pretend to substitute first-hand experience, but a book which relies heavily on the kind advice of experienced experts can hardly provide a handicap. Hopefully *Drive It! Formula Ford* can make the gathering of that experience a little easier, a little less distractive, a little less costly. As more than one racing driver has said when contributing to this book, "The best piece of advice I can offer is 'listen to advice'!"

Typical Formula Ford action. Since 1967, there has really only been one formula where a driver can learn the sometimes spectacular art of single-seater racing.

1 The Formula Ford story

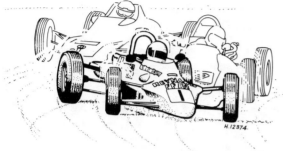

In the Beginning was the word. And the word, as always, was Expense. That age old motor racing problem; afflicting many, dulling the raw ability of most. A problem especially disconcerting to the young and ambitious and British. A problem which was so disconcerting that it sometimes seemed to threaten the very participation of British drivers in future world class racing.

In 1967, of course, Britain could still produce famous sportsmen and women. Only that year Francis Chichester was bestowed a knighthood for his gallant solo voyage of the world in Gypsy Moth IV, while just a couple of months earlier poor Donald Campbell had been killed and his name splashed across newspapers throughout the world, in that infamous accident on Coniston Water.

Even in Grand Prix racing British names were making the headlines. In July of that year, for instance, the Bugatti circuit at Le Mans hosted the French Grand Prix, which was unusual, and no less than six British drivers, which was not. Consider that there were only 15 drivers on the grid, and that a further four of those were from Australia or New Zealand, and the importance of the Commonwealth becomes obvious. Rugged Denny Hulme was on his way to his only World Championship victory in a Commonwealth car, a Brabham, while his closest pursuer was Jack Brabham himself, still building on a sporting legend that would one day bring him a knighthood. Names such as Jim Clark and Lotus, in particular, kept the Union Jack flying high.

But back in Britain itself the signs were worrying prior to July 1967. It sometimes appeared truly miraculous that British racing drivers could continue to reach the summit of their sport at all, let alone in such quantity. Motor

racing pundits looked at national racing, at the so called training ground of tomorrow's Grand Prix talent, and couldn't help wondering how long it would be before the Union Jack slipped down the mast. The problem was frighteningly simple: there was no training ground.

The 250 cc Formula Four had long since died on its feet. Though talent might count towards results in British saloon car racing, it ultimately counted for nothing, not for the serious driver. Only the 1000 cc Formula Three series provided an obvious stepping stone for the starlet aspiring to reach the top. But it also provided drivers with an obvious hurdle — expense — that perennial problem, that great injustice which meant that results would often reflect budget rather than brilliance.

Far, far away from the glamour of Grands Prix and the world of Royal recognition, there was really only one place where a motor racing novice could hope to make an accurate, and yet affordable, assessment of his true potential: there was no shame in admitting that your career had been born out of curiosity at a racing school. The Jim Russell Racing Drivers' School at Snetterton, Norfolk, had already been providing racing driving experience to ordinary people with ordinary means for a whole decade. Along with Motor Racing Stables at Brands Hatch, Kent, it was becoming famous amongst the would-be famous.

Yet even the racing schools were not without their problems. Cost problems, of course. The same essential problem that faced aspiring British racing drivers in 1967, of having to accept the high running costs of Formula Three, or otherwise . . . or otherwise nothing. For racing driver and racing school alike, there was little alternative in single-seaters.

Snetterton, 1969: Formula Ford enters its third season, and still the grids are growing. Nearest to the starter, Tony Trimmer's Titan heads no less than 29 rivals.

That solitary 'option' meant purchasing 1000 cc Formula Three engines at no less than £1,000 a piece, at a time when a brand new Mini would only cost you £650. It meant buying racing slicks at a frightening £80 per set. And it meant that at a racing school, where those handling the cars were inevitably heavy-handed novices, running costs were rising like skyscrapers. High costs in turn meant fewer pupils, smaller profits, even higher relative running costs, and yet higher prices. Already dizzy in the spiral, it seemed only a matter of time before the racing schools would eventually fall down.

More by chance than by planned campaign, Motor Racing Stables found a means of escaping from that price spiral before it was too late. One of the Brands Hatch school's instructors, John Thomlinson, thought that perhaps it might be interesting to replace that expensive 1000 cc race engine with a perfectly standard Cortina GT motor. In his experience, the beginners didn't really need all that race prepared power anyway, and besides, 1500 cc could surely be made to sound better in the school's promotional blurb than 1000 cc. And £65 instead of £1,000 for each engine would certainly sound a lot better to the school's accountants.

The engine was fitted.

After this first step, the next move was logical and likewise economical: the unusual, new-look Formula Three chassis soon had its racing rubber removed, in the place of which came Cortina wheels and Firestone road tyres. Again perfectly standard, and again much cheaper, at £30 per set instead of £80 per set.

While the less powerful engine was, indeed, a beneficial alternative to the 1000 cc race unit, because it gave the novice driver a more easily workable, wider power band, the narrower tyres had their unexpected advantages too. On five inch wheels, the Firestones were obviously more flexible than the previous slicks; more predictable, more familiar in their behaviour, much more prone to sliding and skipping across the track. Much more instructive, in other words, in the delicate art of car control.

Freed from the cost spiral, Motor Racing Stables manager Geoff Clarke surely felt considerable relief. Here was a new car which was not only easier to maintain and cheaper to run than the standard Formula Three machine, but also much more suited to the educational needs of the inexperienced racing driver. Geoff Clarke must have been a happy manager.

Within the next year, 1967, Clarke's almost fortuitous solution to prohibitive racing school costs would have more far-reaching effects than simply rejuvenating MRS's business. Largely as a result of an early discussion with his Brands Hatch neighbour, Motor Circuit Developments Managing Director, John Webb, this simple solution would also rejuvenate British single-seater motor racing.

Immediately, the astute Webb could envisage an application of the MRS type of car on a much wider scale, in public races. Ultimately, he felt it could benefit all those very serious but very demoralised aspiring young racing drivers who decried the costs of Formula Three and longed for an alternative means of illustrating their talent. On both counts he was right.

One man who could recognise the sense of Webb's scheme, and who was instrumental in its launch, was the then Competition Manager of the Ford Motor Company, Henry Taylor. He made powerful illustration of such faith by agreeing to supply to Webb 50 of the 1500 cc Cortina GT engines at the discount price of £50 each, instead of the normal cost of £65. With this helping hand from Ford, Webb would then arrange the construction of 50 cars to accommodate these engines, and market the whole concept. At last he could promise junior drivers a form of single-seater racing that would be relatively cheap and definitely close.

All Webb had to do now was find a constructor for the chassis, and play on the theme of 'the £1,000 racing car'.

All Ford had to do, beyond allowing that initial, favourable transaction, was sit back and hope that the formula would succeed; that it would enjoy a warm welcome and widespread publicity. If it did, then Henry Taylor's total £750 discount would be proven very shrewd indeed: in all that publicity, the new category would be referred to as Formula Ford.

Yet at the very next stage of Formula Ford's launch programme, it met a temporarily worrying hesitancy. Invited by Webb to manufacture what must then have been the largest ever production order for single-seater racing cars, Bruce McLaren turned his back on the idea. He wasn't interested in this new, unproven formula, he said, because there was surely more profit waiting for a racing car manufacturer in Formula B in the United States.

With the unfair benefit of hindsight, we

Part inspiration behind Formula Ford belonged to Motor Circuit Developments MD, John Webb. From his office at Brands Hatch, he can still witness the Ford formula enjoying popularity nearly two decades later.

11

know that McLaren was totally wrong. In declining Webb's order, the brilliant New Zealander made one of his rare and most costly misjudgements.

Lotus Chairman Colin Chapman did not make the same mistake. He could see the great promise of the new formula; he was certain that he could see a means of adapting his current Formula Three chassis, the Lotus 51, to suit Webb's needs. The simple, tubular spaceframe construction would be easy enough to modify; to re-name as a Lotus 31 and a Formula Ford.

In the Lotus factory at Hethel, the idea began to turn to a metal reality.

As the first 50 pukka Formula Fords came off the production line, it was confirmed that conversion of the Lotus 51 was not only reasonably simple, but also cheap. Even cheaper, perhaps, than Webb had originally hoped. Complete with an engine from the batch supplied by Ford, and a gearbox provided by Chapman's factory, the production cost of the finished unit

was just £850. Webb the motor racing publicist had also been correct in his original insistence: he *could* market this as 'the thousand pound formula', and he could enjoy a healthy 17.5 per cent mark up on that first batch of cars as well. It was to the enthusiasm of buyers and seller alike that Formula Ford was launched to its public in mid-1967.

The first race, naturally held at Brands Hatch, was an innocuous enough affair. Formula Ford's very first leader spun off into the barriers after just one lap, and its first winner, one Ray Allen, did *not* go on to immediate international stardom.

Nevertheless, the formula was quite quickly accepted. Here, after all, was what They had all been crying out for: not merely another promotional outburst full of sound and fury, signifying nothing, but motor racing's genuine Fanfare to the Common Man. Whether he wanted fame, fortune, or just plain good fun, the man in the street who was moved by motor racing could now

One of the best known names associated with Formula Ford has been that of racing school pioneer, Jim Russell. Here he keeps an eye on his first ever pupils, in brand new Lotus 51s, from the Snetterton pit wall. Amongst his company, the mechanic in the Dunlop coat is Ralph Firman, later the wealthy director of Van Diemen cars.

A few weeks after the previous picture was taken, the pupils took part in the first ever FF race, at Brands Hatch on July 2nd, 1967. Seventeen years later, the JRRDS resumed its brave policy of holding pupils' races at public meetings, at Snetterton again. Here, the author leads such a race.

participate himself, if he was only prepared to make an effort. *He* could own a racing car for £999; he no longer had to find the £3,200 a Formula Three car cost. Those convenient excuses about the impossible costs of Formula Three, or improbable benefits of saloon car success, or legendary predominance of wealthy Gentlemen Racers, were no longer valid.

Since that significant Sunday afternoon of July 2nd, 1967, 'proper' motor racing has been open to a considerably wider population. Though Messrs Webb and Clarke had probably only *dreamed* as much whilst watching that first, ten lap, ten minute Formula Ford race at Brands, it was indeed the start of something very special. Democracy had at last pervaded the sport of aristocrats.

What Formula Ford may have lacked since in radical technical innovation, as a result of its internationally stifling design restrictions, it has

more than compensated for in the consistent competitiveness of its racing. Every time the starter lets loose another Formula Ford race, you know the racing is going to be as close as a Swedish sauna. Afterwards, panting like tunas who have been on deck for several hours, the drivers will tell you that it was probably just as exciting.

Despite its constant energy, Formula Ford shows no signs of running out of breath. In 1985 the category will come of age, yet it shows no symptoms of weariness other than in general reflection of our frosty economic climate. Formula Ford has survived problems since its initiation, most conspicuously the notorious and costly unreliability of the Renault gearboxes which Chapman persuaded Webb and Clarke to accept as part of the first batch of 50 cars. And doubtless Formula Ford will survive its problem of the moment which, as every team manager will tell

Belgian Claude Bourgoignie was one of Russell's first team representatives. In the very first FF race, he finished third behind JRRDS team mate Malcolm Payne, and the rival Motor Racing Stables car of Ray Allen. Here, Bourgoignie leads another race at Brands, later in the year.

Tim Schenken, another of Formula Ford's early success stories, and one that went all the way to Grands Prix.

you, is the terribly disproportionate expenditure demanded by inconsistent and quick-wearing tyres. Running costs have risen in real terms, but then, of course, they would: though Webb's strong emphasis on economy was more than mere hyperbole at the time, such spectacular cheapness could not be expected to last.

Being founded on low cost, Formula Ford is inevitably accused of high costs each time a new season begins, bringing with it as it will more expensive cars and running bills. The world finds it easier to recognise high cost than it does high technology, and always has done. Only thirteen months after FF's modest christening, *Motoring News* of August 1st, 1968, described the much vaunted £1,000 label of the formula as a point of 'controversy'. On the very same page, Lotus Cars advertised its 51A as, 'Your chance to enter the exciting field of single-seater racing for less than £1,000'. Nearby, Maxperenco Products Ltd offered its Formula Ford challenger, a Dulon, in 'rolling chassis' form for just £625.

Yet journalist Alan Henry could see the other side of Formula Ford's fresh public facade. He observed: 'Clearly there are many cars which have cost more than this sum to bring them to race-winning specification while remaining within the letter of the regulations inasmuch as their basic cost did not exceed the maximum. On the other hand, many of the F3 variants may well have cost over the permitted sum to build, but their cost is almost impossible to assess for this purpose. The question of price and money spent on after-purchase tuning must be sorted out quickly before the whole thing gets out of hand and follows F3's price spiral.'

It was not sorted, of course, and the price spiral had indeed already begun. Poignant justification of that newspaper article's concern could be seen only inches away from it, in another advert. A company called Racing Services, from Hanworth Air Park in Middlesex, explained that it could perform the vaguely defined art of 'Formula Ford Engine Preparation' for £100 — some ten per cent of a Formula Ford's legislated total purchase price, and very nearly double the cost of the standard Cortina engine upon which such wonderful tuning wizardry would take place. It is not only

15

in the 1980s that Formula Ford promises relatively small origination costs to arouse the interest of the novice driver, only to then request largely unexpected running costs, which mean that a rather different kind of interest is shared by his bank manager.

While the opinions of many suggest that engine tuners are controversial, and their objectives nearly always transparently financial, it is indisputable that they are also vital. That's Formula Ford's first fact of life.

In 1983, one leading FF team manager categorically stated that, 'chassis are much of a muchness once you understand them, a driver has either 'got it' or he hasn't, and it's the engine that makes all the difference. It's true — if not always fair — that the good motors tend to go to the good teams with good budgets and good drivers, but a good driver with a bad motor isn't going to be any good at all.''

In 1969, the importance of engines in Formula Ford was already clear. In January of that year, *Motoring News* remarked relevantly: 'The rate of technical progress in Formula Ford is astonishing. Lap times have fallen spectacularly in the 18 or so months of the Formula's existence, while the businesslike attitude of its foremost competitors has brought a breath of professionalism to club racing. Formula Ford is undoubtedly here to stay.'

Indeed it was — and so, too, were the engine tuners. 'The drops seen in FF lap times', observed *MN* correspondent Mike Doodson, 'are attributable mainly to the ability of skilled men to extract more and more power from obstensibly standard engines.' In the 15 years since, a great many skilled men have extracted, in addition, more and more 'folding green'.

Unlike prices, Formula Ford lap times went on dropping. Though they no longer fall in great landslides, as they did in the late 1960s, circuit records are nonetheless subject to a gradual process of erosion. Today it is primarily chassis development, and the often inconsistent trends of

Tony Brise builds on a reputation that would also take him all the way to Formula One, only so tragically to lose his life in Graham Hill's last private aeroplane flight.

tyre technology, that challenge the stopwatch. The engine tuners have indeed performed a skilled task in stretching the capabilities of Ford's 1600cc Pinto engine, but if they stretch it much further it will simply break. As Adrian Reynard's article devoted to Formula Ford chassis design explains so well further on in this book, improvements arrive nowadays in a slimline shape illustrating real depth in aerodynamic understanding. For a humble 1.6 litres, Ford's famous engine might pack a relatively mean punch, but Formula Ford designers are creating cars which pack a still meaner punch through the air.

'Chassis started to get a little bit stiffer, and people started to think a little big about weight', recalls Van Diemen director Ralph Firman of the 1970s, 'but generally speaking the Formula Ford car didn't change for ten years.'

That decade of stagnation is now over. In the typically quiet, understated manner of a man who has little to prove in conversation that he has not already proven in practice, Reynard admits, 'Recently, we've looked much more strongly at the aerodynamics in Formula Ford. It has changed most in that we do a considerable amount of wind tunnel testing, and of course the more we do to our car, the more we understand it, and the more we can improve its efficiency. I think we did probably pioneer a change in Formula Ford concept design.'

That the pioneering spirit still exists is amply illustrated today: straightline speeds go up, and lap times come down. In the mid-1980s, Formula Ford innovation possesses a new found momentum, swept along by a wave of research data blown out of the wind tunnel. It has to be said — and rivals have to agree — that the solitary but strong presence of designer Adrian Reynard has prompted many of the recent technological advances in the formula. In a restless sport, his is a particularly restless genius.

'I have to put simplicity, and ease of maintenance, and 'crashability' high on the list of design priorities', explains Reynard, 'but inevitably people don't buy simple cars if they're not winning. So I feel partly responsible for the escalation in Formula Ford technology, or advanced technology, and I would be the first to

The source of the Formula's title, power from Ford. In the mid-1980s, the familiar 1.6 litre Kent engine was due to be replaced by Ford's new CVH, which at the time of writing was undergoing trial runs in the Jim Russell school cars.

Alongside the tremendous success of FF1600, Ford's 2000cc Pinto is building a racing reputation of its own. This is one of the first FF2000 cars, a Crosslé driven by Derek Lawrence...

agree that it has not made the cars any simpler.

'The object is obviously to produce winning cars, not at *any* costs, but at whatever cost is necessary at the time to produce an advantage over the competition. I am very aware that I must try to keep it simple at all costs. There are certain complex gains that I will never adopt, or will certainly try not to adopt, on my cars. I'll try to be that responsible. Maybe my level of responsibility is a bit more irresponsible than the other manufacturers have been, but that's the way to winning. Even in Formula Ford.'

Winning is usually a result of progress, progress has its price, and price is never popular. It can certainly seem quite horrifying that 'The Thousand Pound Formula' has ballooned so dramatically in just 17 years that a front-running team will now ask for a seasonal FF1600 budget as great as £40,000. More than a few insiders will tell you that the costly fortune of Formula Ford has swollen up so far, like a giant, glistening soap bubble, that it will inevitably pop and spatter, leaving behind it only oily stains. More still will lament the injustice of a formula which nowadays allows to be displayed only the driving talents of those with a considerable budget. But nearly all should remember that, without Formula Ford, there would be nothing at all. In a world of relative values, the value of Formula Ford remains.

Some aspects of rising costs in Formula Ford are doubtless quite inexcusable, but the problems or the politics of the formula should not become the reader's immediate concern. After all, Formula Ford is only a scaled down reflection of motor racing at more senior levels; though FF's scale may have changed over the years, its crucial function has not. It remains the sole single-seater starting point for the ambitious driver. And it should be considered a subtle asset, rather than a painful liability, that the formula not only instructs in the rudiments of car control and competition, but also teaches an approach to the many other

...And this, oh so typically, is Brazilian Ayrton Senna leading a 1982 Formula Ford 2000 pack, chased by Norfolk's Calvin Fish. As the financial gulf between FF1600 and Formula Three widens, so FF2000 serves a greater purpose as an interim category.

challenges presented throughout motor racing. They may seem frustrating and discouraging at the time, but a Formula Ford driver's encounters with inferior engines, or ineffective tyres, or incomprehensible chassis reaction to adjustments, or inadequate finance, can only help him tackle those very same problems as they recur later on in his career, for recur they surely will.

On that premise, this book concerns itself not so much with camber settings and contact-breakers and camshafts, but more with the fundamentals of getting out there in the first place, of getting a car together and getting as much from your budget as you can. Sponsorship traditionally receives superficial mention in books of this sort, but in this one you will find the taboo 'money talk' loud and clear. After all, without sponsorship consideration of such matters as the purchasing of equipment, or preparing the car, or taking technical tips, or choosing the correct chassis and championship, are all mere hypothesis. With sponsorship, the ball game starts, and the technical teaching is best left to your team.

Indeed, the lessons learnt in Formula Ford are so delightfully diverse that, 'It's a training ground for a whole industry now', according to Adrian Reynard. 'It, the only serious starting point for a person wanting a career in serious motor racing — whether it's drivers, mechanics, designers, team managers, sponsorship negotiators, or companies. This one formula has produced a whole new generation of expertise, not just drivers.'

That expertise is often taken for granted, but easier still to appreciate if we remember the formula's innocuous beginning. Once, there were only fourteen drivers in the category, all in Lotus 51s, and all at Brands Hatch. Then Jim Russell and a gentleman called Allan Taylor conspired to produce another chassis, the Russell-Alexis, which opened up the competition to another 50 drivers, and initiated the rivalry between manufacturers. Within months, more cars had come from Merlyn and Mallock, and more budding World Champions had sufficient encouragement to come out of the woodwork. And the snowball has just kep on rolling. As you read this, there are

Another Brazilian youngster who 'made good' in Formula Ford, and who perhaps helped make FF's own reputation so good: one Emerson Fittipaldi in second place at the Mallory Park hairpin in a JRRDS Van Diemen.

more than a dozen different sources producing and perfecting FF chassis, more than two dozen preparation teams devoted wholly to Formula Ford, and more people brave enough to race in the formula than it is practically possibly to calculate. There are literally hundreds of races in a British Formula Ford season, and rather too many championships. And there are even two varieties, now, of what should accurately be labelled Formul*ae* Ford: as a later chapter emphasises, Formula Ford 2000 has grown out of its own Gentleman Racer beginnings and become another solid rung on the World Champion's ladder.

Delete the justifiable superlatives from any description of Formula Ford, and there would be almost nothing left to be said.

Naturally, the Ford Motor Company is delighted with its share in such success. Its Director of European Motorsport, former professional rally co-driver Stuart Turner, declares that Ford is, 'quite staggered at the formula's success. And it's healthier now than it's ever been. Looking at it all ways, it remains the very first form of single-seater racing for anyone heading to the top.'

There are those who will remark that Ford's actual bodily support of the formula has been rather less staggering, and that it required discussion between the President of the European Ford Drivers' Association and Opel, on the highly-charged subject of engine supply and manufacturer rub-off, to prompt renewed assistance from the Ford Motor Company. There are others who would no doubt point out that Formula Ford has never required any form of bodily support, anyway.

Whatever; it was with Ford support that the story could start, and it is with Ford support that the story is guaranteed to go on until at least 1990 for Ford has made a formal promise to maintain supply of its 1600cc OHV Kent engine until then. Ford has also issued financial support for the 1600cc RAC Championship in 1984, and in the same year introduced an FF Race of Champions in 12 different European countries. In 1985, the dozen 'Champions' will meet each other in a Champion of Champions final, which will be held at an important international race meeting, in front of important persons such as Formula One constructors, thus continuing the important role of the formula: illuminating stars on the ascent.

As long as Formulae Ford go on doing that, their future is secure. And perhaps that includes your future, too?

2 Sponsorship

H.12373

It might as well be said right now: the only way you'll ever make a small fortune in Formula Ford racing is by starting out with a big one. It is a necessary evil that money is the root of all motor racing. Whether that implication is one that you love or loathe, you will certainly be obliged to learn to live with it. Even at the most modest levels of Formula Ford competition, 'money talk' can be loud and breathtaking.

Finance is not necessarily the Be All to Formula Ford success, that much is true; but its lack can surely mean the End All. Budget capacity can truly make the difference between winning and losing, and will almost definitely make the difference between your merely sitting on the sidelines or sitting in a racing car. Sponsorship is motor racing's hard case: hard cash, or hard luck.

This chapter could well be the most important in this book to you. Its message is vexing but vital. Only when you have listened carefully to the quoted advice of experts on this subject will you be ready to consider what the rest of the book has to say: if you fail to raise finance in the first place, there is every probability that you will not even have the opportunity to succeed or fail at any other aspect of Formula Ford racing. As a serious racing driver, the need of sponsorship will present you with your first serious hurdle. If you are unable to clear this, it may also be your last.

Let there be no illusions before you romantically turn Formula Ford Dick Whittington. The mythical paving stones of gold are in the main soiled with much the same detritus as are the concrete ones.

The trail of the sponsorship hunter is a long and polluted one. There are monetary mirages that drive you on and on, only to disappear the moment you reach them. Rejection and disappointment hide at every turn. The hunter's path is well trodden, and nearly every little sign of encouragement has been trampled upon before. Rather too often, you will ultimately discover that your commercial prey has already been chased, so rudely and so brutally that it now assumes a stubbornly defensive position at the first sign of other hunters. As a consequence, you will constantly find yourself having to abandon one lead for another, one type of sponsor bait for another. And in each and every move, you will also have to practice discretion: if you do not track down the hunted sponsor promptly and effectively, someone else will.

There must be nothing bullish about your monetary hunt, in fact, quite the contrary; the search for sponsorship is a delicate business. Even the word itself must be handled with care: according to dictionary definition, a 'sponsor' is a 'person who makes himself responsible for another, one who provides support for a cause he believes in, a patron.' But sponsorship and patronage are two very different kinds of arrangements. If you have a patron — that is, a wealthy supporter primarily interested in sharing the excitement of your racing — you are very lucky. If you have a sponsor, you will have to work hard: companies make an investment expecting to see a return. How you may provide such a return, in more tangible forms than mere race success, will be examined a little later.

The sponsorship subject can often seem ludicrous: it is surely the most essential of motor sport's complex ingredients, and yet it is also the most widely misunderstood. Like sex, it is usually very private, often taboo, and yet so vital to the continuation of life. Unfortunately the comparison

With the application of imagination, motor racing sponsorship can cause quite a stir. This is the famous 'small-family car'.

can be stretched to teenage sex; it is practiced with the clumsiness of inexperience, riddled with naïvety, and yet sufficiently exciting and rewarding to tempt short-sighted irresponsibility. The sport is full of self-believing negotiating experts who are better described as self-abusers. Motor racing and marketing are chalk and cheese.

One man who really is remarkably adept at exchanging his Bell Star for a Bowler, however, is 1983 British Sports 2000 Champion, Mike O'Brien. This 30 year old former Formula Three runner is now a professional national racing driver, and a very professional motor racing marketing man. He has succeeded in capturing more blue chip sponsoring companies than there is room here to mention. He attributes that success to planning and approach: O'Brien will be found in company foyers as a meticulously prepared and articulate promotions professional, whereas too many others will breeze through the corporate swing-doors as little more than open palmed racers with a plea for charity.

'It's the first fundamental error', says O'Brien, 'that people underestimate the task. They don't even sit down and think about it long enough before putting the big right foot forward. Just because they're good at running a racing team or good at driving a racing car, they don't

suddenly assume that they can conduct music or write a book — but they do suddenly assume that they're excellent marketing men!'

That is the crux of the problem. Off the track, you are obviously in direct competition with your racing rivals in the search for sponsorship. It is true that, once the racing season stops, the sponsorship season starts, and the competition only gets meaner. But it is also important to realise that your competition no longer only includes other racing drivers or teams.

In your quest to plug into company advertising and promotion budgets, you will have to contend with specialists in selling. There will be other, often more famous, sportsmen and women knocking on the same corporate doors, from sports whose running costs are but a fraction of those of Formula Ford. There could be queues of sports event organisers, offering the potential sponsor the title of an entire occasion rather than a sticky-back label on just one of its participants. They might even be clutching contracted guarantees of television coverage. And there will also be the highly paid and valued professionals: marketing managers and advertising agencies who will be unable to recognise so much as a glimmer of your brilliance beneath a stack of promotion alternatives that will include broadcasting time, and

23

publication space, and billboard displays, and crowded public shows and exhibitions, and promotions at their products' points of sale.

It is not enough, then, to be a more effective promotion medium than the guys you can beat around Castle Combe on a drizzling February afternoon. You will be up against 'the professionals': experts who, during every minute that you are otherwise preoccupied with gear ratios and camber settings, will be applying their experience and imagination to a-million-and-one other lively promotion schemes. Difficult though it is, you must try to fight back with comparable professionalism. If that prospect is one you quite honestly think you cannot cope with, commission someone who can. Someone who understands marketing rather than just motor racing.

Choosing a target company

There is no magic or mystery in obtaining sponsorship. Even motor racing's most famous of 'money men', former Grand Prix driver and World Endurance Sportscar contender Guy Edwards, insists: 'There's really no great secret. The key to

success', he laughs from the opulence of his Chelsea residence, 'is nothing other than a dirty four letter word. Work.'

That work should begin in scrupulous detail months before you go knocking on directors' doors. In this respect it is worth noting that 'the Sponsorship Season' is in fact a fallacy: the hunt should continue throughout the year, in between your racing.

The initial research stage in your plan of attack is as important as any others. Lay a well-founded basement, and you are more likely to be able to build on it. Don't go chasing Golden Geese before checking first whether they have any spare eggs to lay. It is sorely tempting to go rushing off on the sponsorship trail motivated by impatience and intuition, but is probable that you will be charging headlong down a dead-end. Intuition alone is rarely a safe guide, and especially not until you are an experienced hunter.

There are no totally safe guides, of course. You will save yourself a lot of wasted time and effort, however, if you remember to judge what it is you are in a position to offer companies, rather

Through mis-conduct or simple bad luck, you can lose a sponsor far quicker than gain one. According to sponsorship wizard Mike O'Brien, 'You might be asked things such as what happens if you smash the car up. You've got to have all the right answers, and guarantee a service.'

One of few men truly adept at exchanging Nomex for pin-stripes: former Formula Three contender and 1983 British Sports 2000 Champion, Mike O'Brien.

than vice versa. The Bank of England could obviously afford to sponsor a Formula Ford car, but would it want to? How might it benefit? Does it really give tuppence about your startling Silverstone success? Ask yourself questions like these and always give honest answers.

So what companies *could* benefit from an involvement in motor racing? That they will benefit from involvement is the first concept you will have to sell them, and furthermore an involvement with your car in particular, which will have to be the second tier of your sales talk. O'Brien provides succinct illustration: 'It's important to think of the size of the company you are thinking of approaching in relation to the scale of your racing programme. In Formula Ford, you could be offering anything from the local championship to the European series.

'Rothmans, for instance, might seem an obvious choice. They obviously spend millions in motor sport, and billions in advertising campaigns. But they spend that money for worldwide exposure and brand image. They're hardly likely to get that exposure or image if you're trundling

O'Brien in his other 'office'. National Girobank legends feature prominently on car and helmet, but Mike is the first to emphasize that space on the racing car should only be the start of your promotional package.

Packed grandstands, perhaps, but never forget that your car is just one of many. Even when you are winning, race-track exposure probably isn't enough. It is often away from the circuit that you win with the sponsor.

If you can, ensure that your sponsors enjoy the spectacle of racing in comfort — they will be accustomed to VIP treatment. Whilst a luckless Formula Fordster provides the entertainment at Silverstone's Woodcote chicane, sponsors and friends look on from the row of hospitality suite balconies.

Identify your target companies through detailed research and ruthless, self-critical commercial logic. Everyone writes to petrol and oil companies for sponsorship, Julian Bailey's BP backed FF2000 Reynard is a rare exception in getting it: motoring related businesses are not always those most likely to benefit from racing, but they are the ones most heavily bombarded with pleading letters.

around at the back of the Champion of Brands races. And, at the other extreme, the local garage isn't likely to have any advertising budget whatsoever, let alone a budget to contest even the smallest Formula Ford series. So you need to select correctly the level of the company.

'Location comes into it as well. If you're talking to a company whose products make a profit of several million pounds, make sure you know *where* they make that profit. If they're based in Manchester and don't sell anything south of Stoke, they won't see much point in being on the side of your racing car at Thruxton — even if it *is* a winner. The fact that you might be a good racing driver can often be surprisingly irrelevant.'

Look out for new product launches too. If a British company is about to enter European markets for the first time, and if your career could benefit from a season contending the European Ford Drivers' Association races, don't miss the opportunity. It's a tentative link, but links alone always are: they simply give both sides good reason to sit down and talk further, at which point

what you've got to say for yourself had better be good...

'If needs be', advises O'Brien, 'Tailor your race programme to suit the company's requirements. It's not always ideal, of course, especially if you've got your heart set on doing a particular championship. But if your efforts to find backing for that championship have not been successful so far, some races at Silverstone for your Northampton based sponsor are a damn sight better than none at all.'

Adaptability, then, is important. Operating from the office of his Speedsport Promotions company, O'Brien has learnt that ad hoc adjustments to original aims are vital all the time. Each different company has a different requirement and different level of commitment. Some sponsors may only opt for a tiny involvement, taking up more space in a trackside hospitality suite than does their money in your coffers. Tolerate it. No matter how modest a sponsor's involvement may be, and no matter how disproportionate the consequent administration and politics, keep

27

Advertising so blatant it was banned . . .

Facts first. This is not merely a matter of sport, and neither is it a naïve belief that sponsorship is something which verges on benevolence. Far from it. This is business. Common sense commercialism, and nothing else. We do not knock on your company's door with cap-in-hand, and we don't even dream about receiving something for nothing. We wouldn't sell ourselves that cheap.

No. We hope we have something to offer *you*, sir. It will cost money, of course. Effective promotion and corporate image improvement always does. The decision to become involved with us will not be a merely whimsical one. But then neither will be the returns.

When observers describe racing cars as "high speed advertising hoardings", they're not far from the mark — to start with. But the offerings of motor racing sponsorship go far deeper than that. They make the usual static forms of promotion look like a Town Crier in the Satellite Age.

Consumers actually *volunteer* to watch these multi-coloured bill boards. In their tens of thousands they go to the race tracks; in their hundreds of thousands they religiously read about it. And in their millions they turn on their TV sets. The British Broadcasting Corporation will tell you that: so blatant is the advertising on the modern day racing car that this 'commercially neutral' broadcasting institution felt obliged to remove motor racing from our screens in the mid 1970s. It was, they said, nothing more than cheap-cheat advertising. But then the irate viewers' letters arrived by the sackfull. Now, BBC2's 'Grand Prix' programme rates second only to one other on that station, and its tremendous response has justified the return of expensive live transmission of continental Grands Prix on 'Grandstand'.

So the racing car is a billboard, yes. Of sorts. But it offers much more than that; more, even, than its emblazoned colour scheme and badge-bedecked driver appearing on millions of TV screens and newspaper sports pages. Most billboards, remember, are flat and dusty. They are tucked aside in otherwise useless space, left silent behind the vibrant hubbub of everyday life. People simply pass them by.

But not the racing car or driver. These, by vivid contrast, are the focal point. Generating excitement. Stimulating atmosphere and stirring emotion. Bursting with a crescendo of urgency and power. Glamorous, with a youthful, dynamic, dashing image. And, if the progressive sponsor has found the right driver, with media magnetism.

Calvin Fish has that magnetism. We won't dwell on the point in this introductory brochure, because his extensive collection of press cuttings and his peak-time television exposure speaks for itself. From the local newspapers and specialist motoring press to a full colour spread in The Sunday Times Magazine, or from local TV news to a guest appearance on the Top Ten rated 'Jim'll Fix It' programme, Calvin Fish is becoming an increasingly public name. He is a widely recognised Grand Prix star of tomorrow, with considerable public support. The prestigious Racing for Britain scheme alone confirms that: under the auspices of this respected, national scheme to support the most promising young racing drivers in our country, Calvin receives financial assistance from none other than the race spectators themselves. He is *that* talented, that popular.

The physical advertising with car and driver, however, is only the start of it. There is the promotional follow-up to capitalise on. The colourful posters, popular stickers, neat team uniforms, driver's overalls, and team transporter all boast the company legend. There is head-turning exhibition potential in the form of a spare racing car, permanently available for shows, conferences, or even the company headquarters' foyer. An advertising and prestige medium that will actually make people stop and stare and talk.

Consider, too, the implications of a racing backdrop. Motor racing is technically sophisticated. It is innovative, progressive, competitive. It attracts thoughtful connoisseurs rather than rowdy fans, and is an environment bubbling with business contacts. A circuit itself is a refreshingly different, interesting sphere in which to lay the foundations of business in an informal but commanding manner. Hospitality suites provide a luxurious day out for company members and friends. A rare atmosphere in which to openly cheer the corporate image. An impressive base to influence dealings with prospective clients. A symbol of front-of-the-field professionalism.

Once you have identified your targets, approach them in the most imaginative and professional manner possible. The information brochure pictured here was designed and written by the author in 1982 for FF2000 frontrunner, Calvin Fish...

The racing programme itself? After running consistently at the front of the Pace Petroleum British Formula Ford 2000 Championship and European FF2000 Championship in 1982, and winning numerous races, Calvin Fish will be graduating to the Marlboro British Formula Three Championship in 1983. Over half of the names on a current Grand Prix grid have come from this intensely competitive formula in just the last five years. On past form, Calvin Fish will surely be amongst the next Formula One crop.

A hectic 20 race schedule will see the car appear at a multitude of venues throughout our country, spread from Thruxton in Hampshire to Oulton Park in Cheshire, with regular visits to the British Grand Prix homes of Brands Hatch and Silverstone. Indeed, Calvin will actually race in the famous F3 support event at the British Grand Prix meeting; a money-spinning annual highlight which should attract 100,000 spectators at the trackside alone, and one of four or more occasions during the year when the BBC cameras will be present.

And so the reasons could go on. This brochure can only outline the basic principles: the specific concept and niceties of your promotional exercise would naturally be tailor made to suit your own needs. A racing budget can be monopolised by one company, but is frequently shared by several. The annual investment in a media-magnetic front running Formula Three car is not cheap, no. Truly worthwhile success never is. Calvin Fish is not interested in anything other than improving on perfection, and that's why he thinks he could operate well with your company. He has ambitions, not illusions.

If you are only tentatively interested or merely curious, please do not hesitate to pick up the telephone for more details. The more you hear about it, the more you'll agree that it makes sense. Like any commercial offering, that's why Calvin Fish and motor racing survive and thrive.

Thrive with us.

SPONSORS' names and professional showmanship in front of packed grandstands (below). Shooting to prominence (right, top) in Superkarting's top-string Hermetite Zip team. Now he has led the pack in Formula Ford 2000 (right), and is ready to do so in Formula Three, the Grand Prix drivers' proving ground.

Who?

CALVIN FISH. A clean cut, charismatic 21 year old from Norwich in Norfolk. An articulate, intelligent, quietly determined young man.

But not conventional. He abandoned promising 'A' Level studies to become a racing driver. It was a brave gamble widely frowned upon — but a gamble that has evidently paid off. He has been the star of the exciting 150 mph world of Superkarts, and a regular winner in the frantically competitive Formula Ford 2000 single-seater category. In 1983 he will continue his winning ways in the Marlboro British Formula Three Championship — the series that quickly launched the likes of 1981 World Champion Nelson Piquet or leading British challenger Nigel Mansell to instant Grand Prix stardom . . .

...In total, it cost nearly £1,000 to produce, but it also contributed to a professional approach that was vital in obtaining a £90,000 Formula Three budget from BP...

30   Just a small example of sponsorship exposure at the track beyond the actual racing car. Imagination can count for a lot.

smiling. Most sponsors invite other successful businessmen along; many sponsors will privately plan to test the effectiveness of your promotional vehicle first before making a substantial commitment. Whatever it seems they are doing, maintain the cheery public facade, say the right things, wear the right clothes, and ensure that you are always in the right place at the right time. It is all part and parcel of being a *professional* racing driver.

At the early research stage, you could do worse than apply your professional thoroughness to the shelves of the local library. Here, you should be able to draw up a sponsorship 'hit list' and, perhaps just as important, save yourself the wasted time and money of chasing the 'no hopers'. It does not always follow that a company with a hefty annual turnover or profit has an equally gross advertising budget. The rate of a business's growth can often mean more than its present size. Many of the middleweight companies wield the heavyweight promotional punches out of their determination to grow larger; those already large and luxuriant may well have

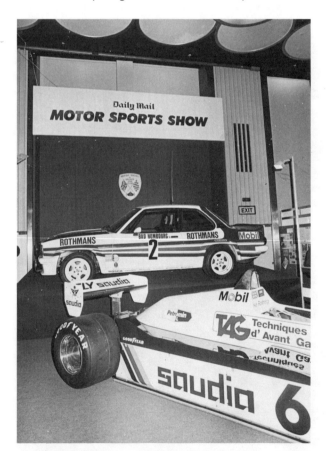

A sponsor's benefits need not stop the moment the race spectators go home. A racing car forms an unusual crowd stopper anywhere, anytime. Trade shows, exhibitions, and even shopping centre displays can all be included in your proposed package.

put on their weight in the wrong places, becoming fat and complacent, or old and conservative. There are several books, such as *Key British Enterprises*, or the list of top UK advertisers titled *The Times 1000*, which are an enormous help in revealing such vital statistics.

The journal of the advertising trade, *Campaign*, is also recommended reading, and a modest investment at 60 pence per week. Its pages will tell you much about the sheer size of company advertising 'spends', their promotional plans and strategies, the approaching new product launches, the precise intention of corporate images, and the partnerships between brand names and their image creators, the advertising agencies.

At a more specialised level, the magazine *Sponsorship News* provides what it describes as 'A monthly update of sponsorship in sport and the arts'. Its editor, Jonathan Gee, has had a direct involvement with motor racing sponsors.

The possession of this type of information cannot be said to have the same effects as holding a magic wand, but if applied in thoughtful ways it can be of significant help. The more you can study such material, the more familiar you will become with the marketing mentality; the better you understand it, the easier you will be able to communicate, or compete, with it. To outsiders, advertising – like motor racing – can appear to be a strange world, made all the more incomprehensible by its specialized language. Make the effort to learn the key phrases of that language, and all your other strenuous efforts at communication with potential sponsors should become more profitable.

Don't, however, place too much faith in your library lessons alone. Be careful to look beyond the stark financial facts and figures. These can only tell how much a company spends on advertising, rather than *how*. Some will concentrate on 'above the line' advertising, that is, media exposure; others will have a more obvious need for 'below the line' activities, such as entertaining clients or instigating trade incentives. All will be sensitively image conscious.

If the promotional package that you are offering a company is comprehensive and imaginative (more about that soon), then the image of motor racing alone will not matter so much. Though the noise and colour and glamour can all be used as strong selling points, your sale should not actually depend on these aspects. Unfortunately, however, the loss of that sale may. Just as the vivid image of modern racing can swing a sponsorship decision your way, so it may also swing a sponsor out of reach. Even skilled experts such as Mike O'Brien are painfully familiar with this obstacle.

O'Brien's encounter with such frustration occurred as recently as winter 1983, when the British Sports 2000 Championship was plainly within his grasp, and when all his existing sponsors had every good reason to be smiling widely from the balcony of his Silverstone hospitality suite.

Amongst those on the outside of O'Brien's promotional programme, eager to get in, was a large national building society. The company's marketing development manager wrote to Mike in October of that year to say that a wealth of previously discussed proposals had been 'accepted, but we shall need some guidance from you as to how we capitalise on the project. Overall we shall wish to be a little more creative on how we maximise exposure, especially through the medium of PR.' The letter writer even took the trouble to offer Mike 'Congratulations on winning the 1983 Championship and good luck on Sunday at Brands Hatch', and enclosed a company tie for the wearing thereof!

Only five weeks later, the building society's attitude had taken a sudden about turn. This time, the marketing communications manager wrote the letter, which started: 'I feel it is fair to tell you as early as possible that we will not be sponsoring you in 1984.'

By way of explanation, he continued: 'This should not be taken as any reflection of the support you have given us or the publicity we have received. The fundamental question is whether racing sponsorship is the correct image for a building society which is the custodian of other peoples money. If we go into sponsorship again, we believe it should be something with a more altruistic image.'

So that was that. At the eleventh hour the unusual, and largely unanswerable question of motor racing morality had been asked. Note that image can be so very important. And remember that the ultimate, solitary opinion of a board chairman — in spite of the cumulative enthusiasm of his marketing management — can be so very important. The lessons to be learnt are plain.

In learning his lesson, O'Brien could at least be thankful that the building society was both honest and prompt in announcing its decision. Not all companies are quite so courteous. Many will spring the bad news upon you only when it is

If the racing car is a mid-week showpiece, then the racing driver must be prepared to play the presentable showman. This is FF2000 Champion Julian Bailey — Dicky Bow and all — accepting a trophy from John Webb's wife, Angela.

The most famous of the sponsorship professionals, Guy Edwards, celebrating a British Formula One race victory in the company of Bob Evans and Desiré Wilson. 'There is no secret to sponsorship', says Edwards, 'other than a dirty four letter word. Work!'

perilously close to the start of the new season. Some will not even remember when the new season begins.

For this reason, as well as others, it is obviously not very wise to pursue one potential sponsor so vigorously that it is to the exclusion of all others. Neither is it very shrewd to count the 'goose's' gleaming golden goodies until they have actually been laid. Too often in motor racing sponsorship, the goose will look all set to lay, only to get up and fly inexplicably at the last minute. And when it does, it will not be gold that drops on your head from a great height...

Making contact

First impressions count. Once you have identified your sponsorship targets, and have honestly convinced yourself that you will not simply be wasting your promotional ammunition by shooting in the dark, you will next have to make contact. It will be a small but significant step: if your initial communication does not open the director's door in the first place, your wonderful arguments about your inspired promotions plan will never get an airing.

That means no grubby letters. Anything that looks like it has been written on the garage workbench with a tube of Gun-Gum will get no further than the secretary's incinerator. Hand-scrawled requests for anything from stickers to sterling are popped swiftly into the proverbial wicker filing cabinet. Almost any letter written by hand will contrast scrappily with all the other typewritten material on an executive desk. Any grammatical errors or spelling inaccuracies could, and should, be recognised as signs of sloppiness. Find someone who can type your correspondence for you, and take the precaution of checking with the relevant company's switchboard operator that you have addressed your letter to the right person.

'A businessman will be used to dealing with businessmen', warns O'Brien. 'That means there is a very real risk of your paperwork looking amateur. I know it's not really very fair, but communication is terribly important in everything in this world. If you can put yourself across well, then you will stand more chance.'

There are other ways of spending a little to improve your chances a lot. Perhaps you should provide your correspondence with the credibility of a printed, personalised heading. Maybe your racing already involves so many financial transactions that it's worth contacting one of those advertisers in the Sunday papers who offer to form a registered, limited company for you.

The construction of a professional image does of course require investment, but in comparison with the sums you will be seeking – or indeed the sums you will soon be spending going round and round in circles in a motor car – this cost is minute. Several hundred sheets of headed paper will cost little more than £30 at a local printer; forming a company does not usually cost much more than £100. Also, think about the business cards you might need after chance introductions, or the separate bank account for your racing activities that will make shorter the annual visit of the tax man, or the answerphone that could capture the impatient or important caller whilst you are out on the sponsorship hunt elsewhere. Think, in other words, as any other self-employed, professional businessman would. That should be exactly what you are.

Not unnaturally, the more you should wish to accumulate, the more it will usually be necessary to speculate, in both time and money. Good-looking stationery is really only a bare essential. In many circumstances, it will ultimately be profitable to invest in a professionally produced presentation package. This could be a loose leaf file with single-page inserts, which can be modified or replaced whenever they become outdated. It could be a shiny-fronted, hard-backed, spiral bound file, with information

orientated solely to the approaching season. It could even be a four- or six-page glossy brochure, with one or both of its sides printed in colour. You might choose to inject some life into your planned sales talk with diagrams illustrating the different levels of a sponsor's returns, or you could project slides to ensure that none of the sport's rich colour and atmosphere goes unnoticed, or present the potential sponsor with artwork illustrating a racing car and driver and team equipment in his company's colours, or instead use a studio photograph of a scaled-down model racing car bedecked in the corporate livery. Yes, one well known veteran of British Formula Ford 2000 even went so far as to paint a *real* racing car in the colours of a potential sponsor, and parked it on the director's doorstep as a dramatic means of introduction! And it worked.

The possibilities, then, are endless. Apply some imagination to your proposals or presentations, be brave enough to put your money where your mouth is, and rest assured that those crucial first impressions will be all the better for it. And if you are whining already that you don't have any money to put where your mouth is, pause for a moment and ask yourself just how determined you really are? When compatriots Derek Daly and David Kennedy found themselves penniless with the next Formula Ford season approaching, in 1974, they put themselves on the first aeroplane to Australia and worked 16 hours per day down iron mines in the outback. How are your efforts comparing?

Whether you finally decide to invest in a

Never make the mistake of assuming that sponsors will come rushing to you, no matter who you might be. The late Graham Hill's son, Damon, made his racing car début in a John Kirkpatrick Racing FF2000 car in winter 1983, surrounded by national TV crews. But by the season of '84, he had written to the letter page of Autosport *pleading for financial support.*

printed proposal or a less glossy, but more personal, typewritten folder, remember that golden rule about professionalism. If you are going to include any photographs, don't rely on Aunt Edna's handshake with the hierloom Box Brownie. If you can handle a racing car but not words, commission someone more literate to write the information to your guidelines. Many of the poorly produced pamphlets that have plopped onto the author's desk, during his years as a staff member of motoring publications, have been more comic than Jasper Carrott. There are racing drivers out there who have a way with words that will leave you wondering whether the human race is not, perhaps, fated to lose the power of communication altogether.

O'Brien stresses this point, though he personally prefers to rely on individually tailored, typewritten presentations. 'Your presentation must be impressive', he urges. 'It must be attractive and interesting if it *is* mass produced, rather than just another time consuming, tedious thing to read. And it must be tailored to be relevant to the company. I've seen some very expensive brochures that the designer — in fact, probably the driver — has managed to make look very ordinary and uninteresting. It's a fact that marketing people are bombarded with very expensive brochures, not from motor racing or other sports, but from people who want to clean their windows, or sell them office furniture. At the end of the day, no matter how expensive it is, it mustn't be merely a circular.'

We all know what we do with circulars.

The possible production expense of many presentations, and the risk of swamping an executive with so much initial information that he is engulfed without trace and never heard from again, mean that the information supplied by an opening presentation must be very limited. Do not waste it. You talk to a board director in a businesslike manner about promotion concepts. You talk about lap records and googlesprockets to a bored director.

Two FF team men who could tell you a tale or two about the demands of sponsors. Robin Green, left, is an accountant by vocation, and says commercial sense is vital in running a team. Dennis Rushen is the full-time team manager, and says, 'When sponsors become part of your racing, so, too, do politics'.

An imaginative sponsorship proposal is important, but never overlook the obvious. The racing car alone does have pulling power!

As O'Brien puts it, 'Too many people stress their own 'achievements', and their own requirements. They tell directors how great they're going to be with their new Van Diemen. Really, they might as well write in Swahili.'

Anything that is not concerned with the promotional package in the writing of your presentation will inevitably be about motor racing. And almost anything about motor racing is a total mystery to many marketing men. Remember the building society's letter with its casual confession, 'We shall need some guidance as to how we capitalise on the project'? It is not unusual. As Guy Edwards also emphasises, 'Each year, you perfect. You learn where the tiniest gaps are in your presentation. You learn not to run with people before they can walk. I think that's maybe where a lot of people in racing go wrong. Because they themselves are involved, they assume that everyone else has their knowledge. And that's a serious mistake.'

Before selling, or introducing yourself, you will first have to explain the great potential for promotion that lies in motor racing itself. Most of the decision makers who ultimately decide their fate of your sponsorship search wouldn't recognise the Formula Ford Festival if it took place on their boardroom table. It is your initial responsibility to make sure that they would. It is one of your most difficult tasks to ensure that none of the strength of your arguments is diluted in its journey between marketing department and managing director. In this respect, more than any other, a pile of professionally produced promotion brochures most certainly has its advantages.

Almost any interested company will ask many simple, but understandable, questions about motor racing. If they do not ask, offer to tell them anyway. The marketing man's silence might simply be an embarrassed one. The most effective presentation or slide show will encompass most of the necessary answers. According to O'Brien, to begin with 'You might be asked things like 'What happens when you smash the car up?', or 'What happens when the engine blows?'. Obviously you've got to explain that you're guaranteeing a service at a fixed cost, with an assurance of your appearance at a certain number of races. You'll even need a sensible agreement as to what constitutes 'a race': it's no good if you go off on the first corner of practice and are unable to make the race, only for the sponsor to refuse to pay. Your obligation is to get the car to the circuit, and get it through scrutineering. But if, in your presentation stage, you are obviously very professional, you might not even be asked these sort of things.'

Other companies might possess a *little* motor racing knowledge; a dangerous thing! Their cross examination might include exaggerated cynicism, to test your response. O'Brien's recommended cure to that little pain' is an invitation to an expenses paid day at the races. 'The races are really very important', he has found. 'Most companies ask why they should come to a race meeting; most of them probably understand golf or horse racing better. But most people also find it very difficult to say no to something for nothing. So get them tickets, get them to a rented hospitality suite drinking your champagne and watching you race, and chat to them in between your time in the car. Suddenly they've got an involvement, no matter how small, and to their surprise they find it interesting. They've got a car to cheer on, someone they know. They'll sit in your car, see that a circuit can be civilised, and notice just how many other sponsors are involved and are there enjoying themselves. You're weakening the resistance.'

O'Brien points out that, in his experience, 'Formula Ford 1600 cars do have a slight handicap, in that they do tend to look so sort of junior in comparison with a lot of the other cars at a race meeting. But the best way around that is to let the bloke you're talking to have a go in one. That soon changes someone's opinion.'

'Entertaining', he says, 'is likely to swing the deal. A very good proposal or presentation is important to create interest in the first place, and in fact it's probably what gets them to the circuit against their natural, and usually mistaken, instincts. But it's once they are there, as a captive audience, that you see the real benefits.

'You have to remember that these people are *used* to being entertained, and that your show must be good and personalised. But if it is, they'll think it's great. People will suddenly start asking you when you're going racing again.'

Keep the sponsor smiling

Tricky to track down, immensely difficult to capture, a sponsor is not much easier to preserve in good health. Popular belief is that, after all those tense months of investigation and procrastination and negotiation, the signature on the contract is a written invitation to rest for a while. Popular belief is also very wrong.

Never forget that the Sponsor is a sensitive species. Its commercial appetite will require constant feeding, its marketing imagination will need lively entertaining. At the trackside, professional standards will have to be comparable with those back at the boardroom. As the person paying the bills, the sponsor will rarely have any doubt that he is Very Important. And as a racing driver who presumably wishes to go racing again next year, you will have to smooth over short-term problems or politics with long-term considerations. Only the satisfied sponsor will be prepared to listen to your ideas again in future. Only one *dis*satisfied client is sufficient to frighten away many others.

There is a good chance that your new sponsor will want to keep on coming to the races. There is a possibility that a sizeable portion of his motivation lies only in his newly laid pipeline to motor racing involvement, which pumps contentment to egos. If you or your team has given sufficient thought to the design, then the sponsor's corporate colours on the racing car and team uniforms and transporter, and perhaps also your overalls or crash helmet, will look good. This colourful company exhibitionism will make the sponsor feel good. You will have stirred up his enthusiasm for racing with the promise that the approaching season will, indeed, be good.

But none of this is good enough. Although most sponsorship proposals begin with the inevitable promise of a colourful, high-speed advertising hoarding, too many also end there. That is inadequate. The offerings to your sponsor should go far deeper than that. When he stands at the trackside and smiles every time your car goes by, it should be because he knows that his attention-seeking billboard is in fact only the beginning of his benefits.

Mike O'Brien emphasises that the appearance of the racing car in competition is only the first part of an effective promotional package. 'You must never forget all those alternative means of promotion that a sponsor can turn to' he warns. 'Compare the costs of your single, little Formula Ford car with a complete team of footballers that includes several well known national celebrities. Compare those big names with yourself, or some obscure Formula Three driver who does the British Grand Prix support race at ten o'clock in the morning while half the crowd is still sitting in traffic jams. That's the big problem. If you leave it at just driving the racing car around, the returns aren't good enough.'

Although the returns will of course seem better if yours is a race winning car, they are still unlikely to be adequate. You do your winning *on* the track to become World Champion. You win with sponsors *off* the track.

'Winning the championship is helpful from the sponsorship point of view' says O'Brien, 'especially if a key part of the sponsor's aim is to enjoy a race winning image. But if the guy who finished tenth in the same series has more marketing ideas than you, and is generally more outgoing and promotable than you, he will stand a greater chance of finding a sponsor and keeping the sponsor happy.'

At Formula Ford level at least, the racing car is therefore not so much the chemical reaction of mixing sponsor and driver, but more the catalyst. 'A racing car forms a very good way of attracting people to the sponsoring company in situations *outside* motor racing' observes O'Brien. 'That's one of the strongest selling points, in my opinion. If a company wants to sponsor a football match, they get everything that motor racing could give them, and possibly more for their money, on the day. But that's the end of it. The match is played and forgotten. But in racing, the sponsor has a car in his livery. He can use it at a business show or an exhibition at the company headquarters, and it will carry on creating interest long after the event is over.'

Such mid-week activities are integral to O'Briens sponsorship packages. 'Nearly every sponsor you deal with will have a dependence on outlets and distribution', he says. 'There's a chain, and every link is important. As I do, you can build your car into that. Put it in shopping centres, tie it up with a whole promotion programme with your sponsors. The more ideas you've got, the better. Think hard how the company can adapt its needs to motor racing. Most companies — whether they've got a retail product to sell to the community as a whole or not — have their own trade; wholesalers or whoever. Make it clear that your car can be used with the trade. You probably won't need too many specific ideas beyond suggesting the principle, because the company will be able to decide how to make it work for themselves.'

Just as it is necessary to make regular reminders about the car's potential applications away from the track, do not assume that the sponsor will know how to maximise his company's participation at race meetings. Encourage the sponsor to make sure his dynamic new image does not go unnoticed, either amongst his clients or within the sponsoring company's structure itself. Most businesses can profit from the implications of a racing backdrop: it can be argued that as a sport it is unique because of its

If there's a space on your car, it can say something!

technical sophistication and commercial undertones. It is not only entertaining (sometimes!), but also progressive, innovative, and superficially glamorous. The hospitality suite provides a novel and emotion charged sphere in which a sponsor may well lay the foundations of business deals in an informal, but subliminally superior, manner. It is also a rare atmosphere in which company members themselves may openly and unashamedly watch their own car, and cheer the corporate image. An impressive base to influence dealings with established clients and possibly win new ones. A vivid symbol of front-of-the-field professionalism.

You will have to match that professionalism, of course. One team manager whose outfit has a reputation for being as professional as any is Dennis Rushen, of Snetterton based Rushen Green Racing. He is not alone amongst teams in understanding that, 'When sponsors become part of your racing, so too do politics. That's no great headache, but it does mean that the novice driver in particular must keep on his toes. Like the team, the driver's got to be switched on to things beyond just racing the car well. You've got to be careful what you say, make sure the truck and the car and team overalls are always neat and tidy, even when the mechanic's just crawled out from underneath the engine! You should have to do this *anyway,* but you have to become more conscious of it. Although you might only be interested in winning the race and becoming World Champion, you'll have a much greater chance of getting that far if you remember you're always representing a company's image.'

The same attitude should still apply after you have packed the racing overalls away. It's that perennial point about professionalism again. There's no need to look like something that's just fallen out of a Hardy Amies window display, but likewise ask yourself whether a company director will really wish for an association with someone who appears to be a mate of Sid Snot.

It is certainly possible to overdo the 'official image': one familiar Formula Three face during the early 1980s achieved notoriety amongst the motoring press for his constant play on his 'lack of finance'. His budget was terribly stretched, he said, as he drove away from the circuit in his brand new BMW. 'Yes, it's even more touch-and-go now', he would say several weeks later, his sun tan hardly faded from his annual pre-season holiday in the Bahamas. He never did understand why the press published few expressions of heartfelt sympathy.

Yes, the press. They'll be important, of course, in your embryonic Formula Ford days. Though it is questionable whether the pen is so much mightier than the sword that it can actually break you, there are many successful modern racing drivers who will agree that it can certainly help make you. As much as a driver's vanity may enjoy media coverage during the days before the novelty of it has worn thin, a sponsor's investment may actually need it. There lies the reason why you should not be embarrassed about working hard to place your face in the newspapers or, better still, on television.

Some larger companies prefer to generate by themselves their own media coverage, linked with their sponsorship. They will often possess more personal contacts than yourself with the relevant trade press and the softer spots amongst the national media. However, you can usually contribute by pushing your name firmly, but diplomatically, in front of motoring writers and local sports correspondents. It doesn't take long to establish contacts, although if you are an absolute pest it might not take much longer to lose them again. The best advice is to always offer a story line, some helpful facts and figures, and perhaps a small selection of black-and-white prints. And remember that warning about hand-scrawled letters and Aunt Edna's arthritis.

If you are a race winner, or possibly even a championship contestant, volunteer information to the news desk the moment your race has finished and your car has passed scrutineering. As a precaution, politely inform the local radio stations and regional TV headquarters of your existence. If you can provide a news angle, it will help considerably. When Norfolk's rising racing stars Martin Brundle and Calvin Fish found themselves in Formula Three together, in 1983, they capitalised on their friendly rivalry. Fish had 'won' Brundle's former sponsor, BP, in his first season in the formula, but in Martin's second season of F3 he threatened to win the championship: *there* was a story line, and it filled acres of East Anglian newsprint. Both became regular voices on local Sunday evening radio, and Fish was invited to write a local news column. By the middle of the season, the two drivers' energetic PR efforts meant that every businessman in the area had heard of them.

Never make the mistake of assuming that the media will come rushing to you. Do not even assume that they know who you are. And do not be afraid to feed the newshounds with even the merest snippets of information, politely, on a plate.

Media space is plainly valuable. Unlike many other benefits resulting from sponsorship, it is also an easily quantifiable value. Maintain a thorough check of the pages when it is possible your name might appear in them, and start a tidy cuttings collection. With another visit to the local library, and the help of a reference book called

Brad (British Rate And Data), it is possible to measure your media coverage in pounds and pence, by valuing it at equivalent advertising rates. As an example, Calvin Fish has made such assessments — he will not vaguely tell sponsors he received 'a lot' of coverage during that season of 1983, but that he received thousands and thousands of pounds worth. £538,000 in fact.

It is true that the out-of-context use of such impressive figures can be misleading, since of course it is usually the driver's name, rather than the sponsor's, which features prominently in such coverage. As O'Brien points out, 'You shouldn't go marching in to companies telling them their own business. I know of people who have told a company 'You spent £15,000 on a full page advert in *The Sunday Times Magazine*, and for that you could have done a whole season with me'. What they forget is that, for that £15,000, the company will have known exactly what sort of audience it was going to reach. With an advert, the company also had the chance to say exactly what it wanted.'

Nevertheless, it is also very true that though the cost of sponsorship is usually fixed, the smile of the sponsor is not. Every fact and figure therefore helps, but racing facts and figures do not always count for very much. Information does, and so too do pages in publications and seconds on the air. A relevant promotional *package* is what matters most of all.

Formula Ford may teach you how to drive a racing car, if only it teaches you about sponsorship too. Who knows, it might even teach you how to make a small fortune...

3 Counting the cost

It hardly needs repeating that motor racing and money are inextricably entwined. But it is very often said that the only substitute for cubic inches is cubic dollars. This is a common catch phrase that is not so much worth remembering as impossible to forget.

Beyond the scrupulously high professional standards necessary in the obtaining and retaining of sponsorship, the allocation of that sponsorship will require careful planning as well. The biggest racing budget in the world will only make a small impression unless it is spent shrewdly. And likewise, a budget that may at first seem impossibly small can often be stretched to perform the seemingly impossible. The manager of the RAM Formula One team, North London car dealer John MacDonald, used to remark wryly that his entire Grand Prix operation ran for a full year on the sort of finances that rivals such as Renault allocated to catering. Take encouragement from his resolute example, and do not become depressed or disinterested simply because the monetary odds are stacked against you. They usually are.

Formula Ford finance, like any other, can mainly be managed by cautious calculation and constant common sense. Though motor racing has its emotive attractions, it will ultimately prove far more rewarding if you actually go racing in a head-over-heart manner. One of the early difficulties in managing your expenditure, however, will be determining just what *is* sensible: there is often an unclear dividing line between hard essentials and frivolous luxuries. The position of this line can vary enormously, depending on the actual size of your budget, and the depth of your racing experience.

Testing, for example, is a major variable.

Hundreds of miles flogged around an infrequently used track on a rainy day will provide little gain to an experienced driver or team, but the same place on the same day could offer valuable lessons to the novice who is unaccustomed to his car, or driving in the wet, or both. Similarly, the thrifty omission of testing is not always advisable: if driver training, circuit learning, or car sorting really are required, then by staying at home your economy will only be false.

Initial outlay is another fundamental consideration that is open to individual interpretation. A second-hand car lovingly prepared and set-up by an experienced race mechanic will often prove more successful than a transporter load of brand new equipment that has to be 'run' more cheaply by a few mates from the local garage.

Even the conveyance of your Formula Ford to and from the circuits could make a significant financial difference, not only according to the proximity of the circuits that you choose to visit, but also depending on the means of transport that you employ. It would probably be more rewarding to spend nearly all of a limited budget on finishing well in a local championship, rather than spreading the money thinly on car *and* commuting only to run further down the field at tracks throughout the country. And though it might be a sore temptation to buy that big, low-price coach you've seen advertised in the local paper, it could be wiser to purchase a more expensive van instead: the bus will give less miles to each gallon and quite possibly more problems with reliability.

Like so many other decisions that have to be faced in Formula Ford, budgeting is largely a matter of horses-'n-courses. The list of complicated variables could go on endlessly. The best advice on wise cost cutting and mistaken false economies comes from those who have already invested in Formula Ford, sometimes with immediate success, but often learning the hard and expensive way. It is not often that racing drivers or teams like to reveal their total initiation and running costs in explicit detail, whether it be for embarrassment of poverty of fear of accusations of excess. But what follows here are three examples of recent racing balance sheets — even though one, from a major professional team, still prefers to remain anonymous! The picture drawn is not necessarily a perfectly representative or typical one, since there is no such thing. What it does show, however, is the two dramatically contrasting extremes of FF1600 racing, and the price of serious front-running in FF2000. The figures alone will provide indication of the financial priorities. You alone will be able to assess honestly where your own monetary requirements might fit in, depending entirely on your individual ambitions and needs. Professional racing ambitions require professional management; racing for fun should cost only what you want it to...

The disconcerting fact that even Formula Ford racing has probably become too expensive for its own good is acknowledged by the growth of a rather different type of FF series: it is called the Pre '78 Championship, and caters for cars of that description and drivers who do not wish to spend a fortune. It is a series whose concept was created by enthusiasts themselves, with their own pockets to protect — a concept that has brought Formula Ford racing back within reach of the 'common man'.

In accommodating well used chassis, the Pre-'78 Championship very quickly dispelled the well used excuses for not going motor racing. It is not only single-seater racing at its cheapest but, being Formula Ford, naturally also exciting. Previously called the Pre-'74 Championship (up until 1984), this series represents value for the sort of money that almost anyone should be able to raise. Here, it is enthusiasm and effort, rather than affluence and ambition, that counts.

The Pre-'74 Championship inevitably became the habitat of those who race purely for fun, whose love affair with motor racing does not quite extend to a second mortgage. More recently, however, it has also had its place for more serious young men — ambitious novices without the finances to enter any other kind of Formula Ford competition at first, but with the sense to appreciate that here is an environment in which they can cheaply develop driver skills and sponsorship relationships.

Economy is the purpose of Pre-'74 or -78 racing, and if you too are unable to afford anything else then it could serve admirably as a starting point. If you do not *want* to become World Champion, it could bring you enjoyment for years.

One competitor who simply seeks enjoyment is Solihull solicitor, 25 year old Tim Elkins. His introduction to Formula Ford was as a voluntary mechanic to the very successful Dave McClelland, from 1975 until his retirement in 1981. Here, Tim gathered the advice and assistance to encourage his own racing activities, and he made a cautious start by completing a course with the Jim Russell International Racing Drivers School. It was an introduction for which he has the highest praise and economic justification. 'Although schools can seem expensive on paper', reasons Tim, 'they offer cheap experience in the long run. It has been said before, but if you cannot afford to go to school to learn the basics, then you probably cannot afford to race.'

'Racing schools are important, in my experience, because they can teach a novice driver the correct technique, and technique is the only aspect of race driving which can be influenced to any great degree. The other necessary attributes of a driver are either there, or they are not. Unless you are one of those rare people born with exceptional talents, I think you are bound to benefit from going to school.'

One immediate benefit in Tim's case was that, once he had eventually bought a Formula Ford, he didn't have to go pounding round and round circuits learning how to drive it. Dictated by finance, he had stretched his Jim Russell course at Silverstone from 1977 to 1980, paid for with money earnt during his summer vacations whilst studying for a Law degree at Reading University. After leaving university, the school experience gave him sufficient confidence to save for, and buy, his own FF car. He raced this with above average results in the Pre-'74 Championship in both 1982 and 1983. (As a natural progression, he planned to enter the newly introduced Pre-'78 FF2000 series in 1984.)

Before a driver should even think about hunting sponsorship, the initial capital outlay poses the first problem. As Tim observes: 'It is really up to you to make the effort and buy your car, and start off under your own steam. After that, however, it should be possible to find a couple of local businesses who will, say, give you £20 each per race. For many drivers in the series, this is literally the difference between being able to compete or not.

'The average club competitor *should* be able to go out and find some money for running his car. It is never easy, but frankly there is a world of difference between getting £30,000, and obtaining a few pounds per race towards entry fees and petrol. But when you are starting out, it would be wrong to think that you have much chance of

Cheap thrills: solicitor Tim Elkins provides encouraging proof that it is possible to go Formula Ford racing for as little as £65 per race, thanks to the Pre '78 series.

finding someone to buy your car for you. There is a big difference between getting, on the one hand, money towards running costs and, on the other, your capital equipment bought for you.'

Tim's capital equipment did not, however, require a frightening initial outlay. 'I was fortunate to be able to buy a complete car with engine and gearbox, and a trailer, for £1,000 from someone who wanted a quick sale. You'll see Pre-'74 cars advertised in the classifieds in *Autosport* for up to £1,800, and of course these do not always include a trailer, which can cost from £100 upwards second-hand. It is best to buy a complete car if possible, because if the chassis and engine and gearbox are purchased seperately they can prove more expensive. Second hand 'boxes are particularly rare, and tend to cost £400 plus.

'The best time to buy is at the end of the season, and I found my car by going to the Pre-'74 Festival and asking just about everybody in the paddock whether their car was for sale! One thing I was trying to buy was a common marque, as otherwise spares can be a problem — and it helps a lot to have readily available setting-up information too.'

One thousand pounds, then, and Tim Elkins was on the road. But before racing a car you will also need to dress appropriately, and to obtain club membership, medical certificate, and licence. Detailed advice on such paperwork is provided, at low costs and to high standards, by Formula Services, whose proprietor Val Adaway is listed in the Business Directory at the back of this book. The total cost to Tim in obtaining such accessories was £130 — again, a far cry from the sums spent by serious professionals in the top championships, but nonetheless a very encouraging indication of just how cheaply you can start Formula Ford racing. A look at the budget analysis of FF2000 pacesetter Calvin Fish, a few pages ahead, shows that driver's equipment can cost as much as £825 or more! At the other end of the scale, Tim 'was fortunate to be given a helmet, and I bought all my racewear from the person who sold me my car for an additional £60. This', understates Tim, 'is well below the cost of new items.'

Once more, initial expenditure on car and clothing depends entirely on personal requirements. The three-layer Simpson suit that Calvin Fish invested in was justified by the extensive racing mileage he covered in the season, with its consequently greater risks, and his basic philosophy to do all things very professionally. A dozen races in the pre-'78 Championship will obviously present rather different needs.

Likewise, the equipment required to run the car can vary enormously, and the safest guideline is to simply buy what you can afford. Elkins received eight tyres with his car — all worn-in, of course! — and bought another four, also partly worn, for £12 each. The analysis of a top FF1600 teams expenditure in this chapter shows that tyres may cost rather more: £190 per set, or very nearly £50 each. Remember, too, that such a team would ideally don new sets every few races, and quite probably even more frequently under current circumstances. 'We'd normally manage on

Calvin Fish's philosophy was to 'do things properly', and in the long-term it paid off: Calvin ran an FF2000 Van Diemen from his own, Snetterton based workshops in 1982, and wound-up second in both the British and European Championships.

about 15 sets for 35 races' said the anonymous team accountant, 'but because the present tyres are so inconsistent in quality, achieving the perfect set-up for the car throughout the season could need as many as 50 sets!'

Yes, that *is* a conceivable £9,500 per season on tyres alone.

Mr. Elkins' rubber costs are altogether more comprehensible. Twelve tyres lasted him a full two seasons, at an average of about £50 per year. But there is a rub: 'As you can probably guess, I had to juggle them around a lot, and by the end they were all virtually bald and a bit lethal in the wet!'

The price of rubber naturally leads us to the price of running a car in general. The spares and repairs included in Tim's listed 1982 season were largely associated with engine wear, but even so he managed with just one motor and a bill for less than £200 in maintenance. The components of such upkeep were: gearbox bearings, £8; new piston, fitted, £56; new piston ring, fitted, £20; brake pads, £16; water gauge, £10; oil gauge and line, £15; oil pump repairs, £20; mirrors, £15; spare wheel for trailer, £6; welding, £10. This represents a grand total of £176.

In addition, the 'sundries' mentioned in the table included such accessories as plugs, points, WD40, polish, tank tape, brake fluid, tyre changes, and the like.

The engine itself will hardly have been the most powerful in the Formula Ford world, but for Tim's purposes it was sufficient and reliable. 'Unless you are particularly unfortunate or prone to blowing engines', he says, 'you can spend as much or as little as you like. At the top of the scale, some drivers like to have their engines rebuilt after perhaps every three races. Otherwise, the tuners recommend 800 to 1000 miles, which means that, for the average competitor on a tight budget, a fresh engine should last a whole season. It'll obviously be a bit tired by then, but it all really depends on what you can afford to spend.'

A similar *ad hoc* logic applies to other running costs and spares. Tim reiterates that, particularly with dated second-hand machinery, the extent of costs depends partly on the make of car that has to be maintained. 'In Pre-'74', he explains, 'spares are usually found quite easily, often from the manufacturers themselves, for the more numerous cars such as Dulons, Royales, Eldens, and Merlyns. But if you own a 'one-off', you may well have to order the special fabrication of parts. It is extremely useful to find someone locally who can help you, such as a small engineering firm. For instance, I twice managed to get a broken magnesium upright welded, whereas a new one would cost £80 or so.

'If you can also find someone to make fibreglass body panels for you, that's another way of avoiding manufacturer prices. It's obviously up to the needs of the individual, but little things like that really do add up.'

They add up, in fact, to a startling contradiction of the widespread and off-putting image of Formula Ford as a '£10,000 to £30,000 per season' type sport. Tim Elkins only received £235 sponsorship during 1982 — rather less than the price of a professional gearbox rebuild — and yet his total outgoings, which included running costs *and* initial capital outlay, reached only £1,919. Even taking into consideration expenses such as entry fees and travel, his average cost per race was only £65. What further encouragement do you need?

Tim Elkins' racing costs
(Pre-'74 FF1600)

Initial capital outlay

Car, gearbox, and engine (including trailer)	£1,000
Tools	£ 25
Tow bar	£ 50
Battery charger	£ 10
Setting-up car	£ 20
Tyres (4)	£ 48
Overalls, helmet, etc.	£ 60
Battery	£ 25
Licences	£ 50
Club membership	£ 15
Medical examination	£ 5
Sundries	£ 50
Total	**£1,358**

Running racing car

Depreciation over one year (approx)	£ 100
Entry fees (10 races)	£ 260
Testing fees (2 sessions)	£ 40
Petrol (including tow car)	£ 180
Garage hire	£ 100
Oil	£ 25
Spares	£ 92
Total	**£ 797**

Engines

Spares costs	£ 84

Sponsorship and prize monies

Sponsorship	£ 235

Total cost

Total *running* cost	£ 881
Minus sponsorship	£ 235
Overall running total	£ 646
Average per race (10 races)	**£ 65**

Take a deep breath before venturing any further: the financial figures that follow do not make for light reading. If the economies of the Pre-'78 series offered all the encouragement that you need, then look at the next budget in the chapter for immediate disillusionment.

At the front end of the grid, Formula Ford 1600 racing is quite simply a serious business. Its costs, like its pressures, are high. Success is generally small — there can only be *one* winner per race or championship — yet investment is always large. So large, in fact, that the team who provided the balance sheet here insists on remaining anonymous. Formula Ford winning is now such an expensive satisfaction that the team readily confesses its fear of frightening people away...

There is one important point about professionalism to remember, however. It is big budgets that invariably lead to big success. The type of FF running costs reflected here have been known to cultivate the type of driver success that truly helps to pave the way to Formula One. Although it would be wrong to assume that all professional preparation services cost as much as the total given here (or indeed that all cars running from the same workshop would necessarily cost the same), it would be equally misguided to think that shoestring spending can lead to 'big time'

results. The figures shown are intended to illustrate the price of peak professionalism in Formula Ford 1600. Nowhere else is it likely that FF1600 will cost much more, but nowhere else is it likely that the chances of driver success will be much greater.

Superficially, the initial capital outlay of a team-run driver is unlikely to differ to that of a privateer: both will first need a car, engine, essential spares, racewear, tools, and some kind of transport. But the difference in *how much* the team driver and privateer spends on such items is likely to be marked. The driver whose sponsorship affords a seat with a team is usually the driver who can also afford to purchase the best equipment available. Because of this, the costings that follow include initial investment in a brand new car at 1984 prices, plus two engines in case of pre-race breakdowns. The £1,200 noted is only sufficient for truly essential spares, such as the nose-cone and wheels which are most vulnerable in skirmishes; many teams and individuals prefer to live in the knowledge that the replacements available for emergencies are more extensive.

The constant difference between a privateer effort and a place in a team is service — and to the team driver, that not only means the provision of professional personnel and expertise, but also technical facilities. It is interesting to note just

Racing costs depend very much on individual needs. The professional preparation team that volunteered the FF1600 costs shown in this chapter includes a three-car, £20,000 transporter as part of its services. Other drivers will manage happily with somewhat cheaper means of car conveyance.

how much such facilities are worth: according to the race track based team whose costs are analysed here, workshop machinery and tools would demand a current capital investment of £16,000. In addition (though perhaps somewhat excessively at Formula Ford level), the team's three-car transporter cost another £20,000.

'You *could* buy a second-hand truck for about £500', observes the team accountant, 'but it would be really clapped out, and quite possibly unreliable and expensive to keep going.' At the front end of the grid, words such as 'clapped out' and 'unreliable' should not even enter the racing vocabulary.

The other items of team expenditure are largely self-explanatory. The 25 races contested is typical of a leading British championship entrant, whilst the test mileage is simply essential to remaining truly competitive at a level where the chief opposition may include factory run, 'works' cars.

The tyre expenditure listed, at £2,850, assumes use of 15 sets at £190 per time. This, however, also assumes normal wear rates. At the time of writing, reminded the team, 'wear rates are so high and tyre quality generally so inconsistent that many more sets could be needed, particularly if it really is the team's job to win at all costs. As many as 50 sets might be needed!' Sad to say, this represents a possible further cost of some £6,650. Even allowing for the team's likely exaggeration as a means of protest, the point should be taken: financial demands can be enormously flexible, and potentially enormous.

A conspicuous feature in the costings list is driver error. Also variable according to luck and judgement, the expense of accidents must be anticipated in the original budget plan. At worst, consider such expense as an investment in experience – the more experience you have, the less excuses there should be for excursions into the scenery. At the front of the pack, such excursions typically cost £1,200 in miscellaneous spares during a season, and a further £3,000 in bodywork and chassis damage. The average shunt at team level apparently costs no less than £500. It is conceivable, though, that the bigger the available budget, the smaller will be the driver's safety margin...

Top team's racing costs
(National championship FF1600)

Initial capital outlay

Car, gearbox, two engines	£10,000
Tyres (two initial sets)	£ 380
Racewear and admin. sundries	£ 500
Total	**£10,880**

Running racing car

Depreciation over one year (approx)	£ 3,000
Entry fees (25 races @ £35)	£ 875
Testing fees (25 sessions @ £32)	£ 800
Race petrol	£ 220
Testing petrol	£ 500
Tyres (15 further sets)	£ 2,850
Typical spares	£ 1,200
Typical accident costs	£ 3,000
Consumable materials	£ 800
Workshop & admin. overheads	£ 1,600
Team race accommodation	£ 1,000
Mechanic's wages	£ 6,500
Other wages	£ 3,000
Total	**£25,345**

Engines

Depreciation on two engines	£ 2,000
Rebuilds	£ 2,500
Gearbox rebuild	£ 300
Total	**£ 4,800**

Transport

Transporter, all running costs	£ 2,200
Collection of engines, etc.	£ 1,000
Total	**£ 3,200**

Total cost

Total cost (charged to driver)	£33,345
Average per race (25 races)	£ 1,333

It often follows that the larger the category of racing, the larger its costs. Formula Ford 2000 is, alas, no exception. Although the somewhat bulky Ford Pinto engine is only 400 cc bigger than the Kent or CVH motors, the two-litre Ford racing formula itself allows much greater scope than FF1600 for technical initiative. The driver and team must extract the most from slick racing tyres and adjustable aerodynamic wings, additional complications which inevitably add to the expense. Similarly, the ever-increasing competitiveness of FF2000 also pushes up costs. FF2000 is a faster, sometimes more colourful formula than its 1600 cc cousin, and at its most professional level will cost as much as 70 per cent more.

One of *the* most professional runners in FF2000 during the early 1980s was Norfolkman, Calvin Fish. The former Superkart star switched from FF1600 to 2000 as soon as he could, primarily because his previous racing experience had incorporated 'real' racing tyres and wings. Fish's in-car comfort in FF2000 was amply reflected in his results: during the 1982 season, he was the only man to challenge the worshipped Brazilian, Ayrton Senna. Despite a sluggish start to that season in an uncompetitive works Royale, and despite running for the very first time from his father Roy's own Snetterton based workshop, Calvin finished a fighting runner-up to Senna in both the British and European FF2000 Championships.

Before switching to a Van Diemen, Fish's initial works Royale seat meant that he incurred no chassis costs during the first six races. It is also important to note that, because of his competitiveness, his tyre expenditure was not exactly typical of an FF2000 front runner either: although Calvin actually used 25 sets of tyres throughout the year, trade support from Dunlop meant that he only had to pay for five sets. At £294 per set, this represents a substantial saving of £5,880.

Amplifying the value of Dunlop's assistance, Fish also conducted test sessions on behalf of the tyre company, for which he was paid a total of £1,955. Likewise, his abilities as an analytical test driver were employed by Van Diemen, and brought a further £750 income. It must be appreciated that such attractive figures are rare, and that few drivers will be paid for their testing abilities at such an early stage in their careers.

Similarly, it was chiefly because of Fish's ability to run at the front of the pack that he received £950 support from the Racing for Britain scheme. In total, his trade support and testing fees were worth a considerable £9,535.

Fish's brave privateer effort also presented its disadvantages. In choosing to run from his own premises, he had to accept the initial capital investment in a van and transporter, as well as the constant costs of employing and accommodating team personnel throughout the season. At any other, established team, equipment costs would be 'hidden', and team overheads invariably shared with one or two other drivers.

Another sizeable portion of expenditure is accounted for by engines, both in purchase and running costs. Although the acquisition of four motors may at first appear excessive, it is really nothing more than a reflection of the investment that is necessary to win races — it is of poignant interest that these engines came from no less than three different tuners. In searching for optimum engine quality, Calvin Fish Racing found that prices varied from £1,897 to £2,556. Between them, the engines required nine rebuilds, at an average of £543 each time, and at the end of the season their depreciation represented a hefty £5,645. Three motors could be sold for a total of £5,175, but the fourth had completely destroyed itself. In planning your budget, it is always wise to anticipate a certain amount of mechanical misfortune. The less you are prepared for breakages, the more unfortunate they will be.

Because his approach to racing is in every sense professional, Calvin chose to invest in a high quality image, and safety, in race clothing. Particularly when compared to Tim Elkins' £60, Calvin's £825 tab seems a little frightening: again, it is the crucial difference between racing in Formula Ford for fun, and racing as a committed professional.

Itemised, the racewear bill consisted of: XFM1 helmet, £195; Simpson three-layer suit, £430; Adidas boots, £70; Simpson gloves, £60; and underwear at £70. (Always protect your valuables!)

Next listed, the 'essential spares' were precisely that: just two nose-cones, for £195; two-and-a-half sets of wheels at £1,065, which could permit experimentation with different tyres; and £180 for two sets of front wings, which are usually the first things to suffer in a contretemps.

Entry fees today form only a tiny fraction of the overall racing expenditure, but it is worth remembering that racing abroad can prove much more costly. In Britain, Fish's entry fees covered 21 races, at £35 each time; in Europe, a further £420 only brought him to the start line on six occasions, at £70 per time. Continental outings naturally also demand much larger transport and accommodation costs, although it has to be said that they are also much more fun.

Unlike the previous FF1600 team analysis, our examination of FF2000 finances also illustrates income and prize money. In total, this was worth £1,146 to Calvin Fish for each race — above all else, it is a convincing endorsement of the long-term value of investing whatever is necessary to be successful in your racing, and Doing the Job Properly...

Calvin Fish's racing costs
(National and European Championship FF2000)

Initial capital outlay

Car and gearbox	£ 6,440
Four engines	£ 8,585
Transporter	£ 4,000
Van	£ 3,519
Tools	£ 500
Gear ratios	£ 300
Tyres (2 slick sets, 1 wets)	£ 900
Racewear	£ 825
Essential spares	£ 1,440
Total	**£26,509**

Running racing car

Depreciation over one year	£ 900
Entry fees (27 races)	£ 1,155
Testing fees (40 sessions)	£ 1,000
Race petrol	£ 250
Testing petrol	£ 900
Tyres (5 sets)	£ 1,470
Typical spares	£ 1,400

Accidents	£ 400
European Ford Drivers' Association registration	£ 190
Team race accommodation (driver and mechanic)	£ 2,000
Mechanic's wages	£ 3,000
Other wages	£ 320
Signwriting	£ 400
Formula Services paperwork (Handling of entries, ferries, commentators' sheets, etc.)	£ 250
Total	**£13,635**

Engines

Depreciation	£ 5,645
Rebuilds	£ 4,890
Total	**£10,535**

Transport

Running costs	£ 2,000
Repairs	£ 400
Depreciation of truck	£ 1,000
Depreciation of van	£ 1,334
Ferries, visas, etc.	£ 1,000
Total	**£ 5,734**

Total cost

Total running cost (excluding capital outlay)	£29,904
Average per race (26 races)	**£ 1,150**

Team income

Polycon Packaging sponsorship	£17,250
Racing for Britain	£ 950
Hiring out car	£ 5,245
Tyre testing	£ 1,955
Van Diemen testing	£ 750
Hiring out engine	£ 546
English prize money	£ 1,305
European prize money	£ 1,790
Total	£29,791
Average per race	**£ 1,146**

4 Going to school

H.12373

Probably because racing drivers are not generally known for holding a low opinion of themselves, racing driver's trainers are hardly known at all. There is simply no demand for them. Although the richly rewarded stars of high-pressure sports such as golf or tennis are unashamedly dependent on the critical analysis of their trainers, racing drivers seek little constructive criticism. Man hours and monetary millions are devoted to the improvement of cars, yet barely a moment's thought seems to be allowed for the refinement of drivers.

Experts in other sports would no doubt suggest that this attitude is strangely mistaken, if not truly conceited. As a novice in motor racing, you cannot afford to be either. The willingness to learn can be as important as the lessons themselves.

Already in this book, one particular lesson will have become acutely obvious: that is, natural ability as a driver is often not enough by itself. There are too many other demands and disciplines which must complement your driving talent. If, indeed, there is a talent...

Until now, we have conveniently taken for granted the aspiring Formula Ford driver's aptitude behind the wheel. In your own opening moves in the game of motor racing — in buying an introductory book such as this, or perhaps even in buying or building your first competition car — you will probably have taken your ability for granted, too. After all, no-one will devote effort and money to a sport without believing that it will bring a certain amount of success. And besides, you probably *know* that you are comfortably confident at the controls of a motor car, and that your skills are quite plainly superior to those of your fellow road users.

So far, so good. But just how good are your driving skills really, if assessed in a more relevant context? We all know that many of the motorists cluttering up our highways and byways found their licences in the bottom of a Cornflakes packet, just as they all know in the Local of your record breaking run from Little Piddle to Chipping Sodbury. All very encouraging in its own limited environment — but pause for a moment and ask yourself whether foolhardiness on the road necessarily promises flair on the race track. It is rarely the case.

That is certainly not to say that a belief in your own ability should be immediately abandoned. Far from it. Confidence can be a considerable asset in the cockpit of a Formula Ford. Mis-placed confidence can be a considerable danger. Many an Ace from the back-roads has ploughed his entire life-savings into a Formula Ford, only to promptly plough his Formula Ford through several layers of catch-fencing. More still will tell how they have 'raced' faster cars on the road — only to be ridiculed by much tamer vehicles on the track. A few minutes in a Formula Ford can shatter many years of romantic illusions.

A few days spent at a racing drivers' school can provide the novice with 'insurance' against such disappointing debut disasters. It very obviously makes sense to test your potential ability first, before making the heavy commitment that any sort of competition car requires. It also makes sense to test that aptitude as honestly, and relevantly, as you can. Again, it is the racing schools that can provide the novice with the answer: here, you may see how your driving talent really compares, alongside drivers with similarly limited experience and unlimited ambition.

Such comparisons, it has to be said, are not

Going to racing school means serious 'classroom' lectures as well as 'practical experiments' on the track. This is the Jim Russell School's MD, John Paine, discussing a student's problem at the Snetterton Esses. Thorough analysis of each driver's faults at every corner forms the basis of a truly instructive course.

Start young, you won't regret it!

infallible. Most schools only allow their pupils to exploit about three-quarters of a Formula Ford's ultimate straightline performance. (Attend a school, and witness just how much there is to learn if racing driving is to be managed *properly*, and you will understand why.) Likewise, most pupils will only exploit about three-quarters of their own ultimate potential within the first week in a Formula Ford. Naturally, some embryonic racing drivers will develop more rapidly than others in the early stages. But so far as such unavoidable factors will allow, a racing drivers' school will tell you much, much more about your real aptitude than any previous experience in a road car.

This valuable opportunity to measure talent and adopt the *right* habits at the very start of your career is offered by an increasing number of racing drivers' schools in Britain. Some offer a greater variety of course and cost options than others, and some will inevitably be more beneficial than others. All will be of some value to the novice, unless his natural driving ability is quite extraordinary.

It would be a brave man who suggested that one particular racing drivers school in Britain deserves special recommendation. In essence, they are all of reasonable standard, since otherwise they would not survive. There is one, however, which surely enjoys more worldwide recognition than the others, and which has been longest established: ever since 1957, the Jim Russell International Racing Drivers School has introduced young men to motor racing from all corners of the earth. Amongst those adventurous foreigners, one or two have even attained the fame and fortune that they originally dreamt about. There is one, called Emerson Fittipaldi, of whom you might have heard...

The Jim Russell school is very much like the others in that it places great emphasis on smoothness and safety, leaving the speed to follow naturally with time. The JRRDS is also typical in that its instructors emphasise: 'Your greatest challenge on a training course is yourself. Your efforts should be guided by your personal standards, your speed limited according to your own comfortable limits. It is your driving that counts, not how it compares to that of your course colleagues. And it is by judging those personal

Driver's eye view. A slimline FF1600 cockpit, attended in a typical racing 'laid back' position. The central tachometer dominates the instrument display – and disciplines the driver during a school course. A common beginner's difficulty is the restrictive room for wrist movements with the gearlever, positioned on the right hand side, very near to the cockpit surround.

standards at the start of the course, and then again at the end of the course, that you will be able to judge the school's value.'

It is, then, a test of personal standards. A racing drivers' course, like the motor race that may be offered at the end of it, is a very personal experience. The fascination of its constant, day-by-day challenge can hardly be described in a book; the consequent sense of achievement really does have to be experienced to be appreciated. And at the JRRDS, for example, the colourfully cosmopolitan company and the infectious sense of occasion are ingredients for which words can do little justice.

Because it is such a personal experience, the author spent eight days with the Jim Russell International Racing Drivers School as a preamble to writing this book. It was a course anticipated with some cynicism, but completed with a great sense of regret. Like all Good Times, it passed too quickly, finished too soon. What follows is therefore almost by necessity a slightly personal account of a very personal introduction to Formula Ford. Going to school made the international renown of the JRRDS easy to understand, but, more importantly, it also illustrated the concept of racing drivers' schools in general. It is a concept that all but the extraordinarily gifted cannot afford to ignore.

Jim Russell International Racing Drivers School

Romantic notions about the life of a racing driver dissolve immediately, in Snetterton's piercing rain. Any further ideas about actually *being* a racing driver, if only for the week, are washed away just as promptly. Chief Instructor John Kirkpatrick is not going to be impressed by young men holding helmet bags and wild ambitions. His introductory speech in the Jim Russell Racing Drivers School is nothing if not honest and factual. Hard facts, about a hard sport.

Instantly stripped of their dreams, the twelve gathered racing drivers suddenly become school-boys. They listen to the instructor attentively, look at each other nervously, fidget uncomfortably. This isn't going to be any picnic.

'If any of you sitting there expect to call yourself racing drivers by next Sunday tea-time', warns Kirkpatrick in his crisp, Scottish way, 'you might as well leave now.' In the startled silence, no-one moves.

'And if any of you think that driving a Formula Ford car consistently quicker than we recommend is going to impress anyone, you'd best think again. By the end of the week, you will have learnt a lot, and your driving will have improved a lot. But you'll have a whole lot more to learn besides. What we give you here is your first experience of

From the first braking and gearchange point, through the entire cornering sequence to changing-up again, accuracy is the aim of racing schools. Here, Chris Skellern's proximity to Donington kerbing shows why...

... Whilst rather further away from the corner's clipping point, another Formula Fordster illustrates the temptation to exceed personal capabilities. The progressive nature of a racing school means that such limits can be approached gradually, safely, and neatly. With the neatness, they say, speed follows naturally.

The dividing line can be very fine between controlled determination...　　　　　　*... and disaster.*　　55

The most famous 'headmaster' of them all: Jim Russell watches on as a pupil makes his approach to Snetterton's tricky Bomb Hole. The former British Formula Three Champion still takes a considerable interest in the progress of his school's pupils, although the responsibilities of Chief Instructor belong to professional racing team manager, John Kirkpatrick, below. Here class is in session with 12 pupils and no less than 5 instructors.

Formula Ford, conducted properly. That means there'll be no bad habits, no wild nonesense. From beginning to end, you must never forget that in overall terms you are *always* inexperienced. Even World Champions can further the bounds of their experience. Even World Champions can make some pretty damn silly mistakes through *in*experience. Experience lets you put the car into a situation, knowing that you can get out of it. Inexperience is doing the same on a wing-and-a-prayer. You'll be allowed to do *nothing* on a wing-and-a-prayer this week.'

So the scene is set. The school discipline is strict, its standards high. Not least, the Managing Director, John Paine, must put on a good show on Sunday for then, at a public race meeting, the students will race together. 'We don't just expect high standards', Paine admits, 'we demand them. If a student doesn't generally see things our way, we find that he doesn't learn much either. And that's a shame, because most people who come to a racing driver's school have been sensible and honest enough to admit that they don't know all the answers. None of us do.'

According to the entertaining Kirkpatrick, his students 'will know 70 per cent of the answers' by the end of the week. Logically enough, he therefore reasons that they shouldn't go into the race intending to drive at 100 per cent of their abilities. 'Err on the side of caution.' he advises, and throughout the week that message echoes around a dozen helmets. Mistakes simply *aren't* allowed.

Minor mistakes, however, are common place. Even after walking the circuit and examining each of Snetterton's varied corners independently, the task of lapping proves surprisingly hard. Turning-in points are made too early, gearchanges too late, heel-and-toeing clumsily, constant radius grips of the steering wheel inconsistently, power application too suddenly.

At just thirty miles-an-hour, piecing the jigsaw together is a challenge. At the circuit's edge, it is slow-motion farce; at the steering wheel, it is unexpected hard work. The whole point of the course quickly becomes clear: clean, accurate race driving just doesn't come naturally. The Canadian pilot on the course remarks how surprised he is at the mental commitment required. The professional Portuguese rally driver reckons he's found ten seconds per lap simply by appreciating the value of smoothness. The Californian businessman is almost in tears when he has to leave for New York mid-way through the lapping sessions. The South African student shakes his head in sympathy. 'I've waited 21 years for this', he says quite ruefully. 'I would have let the business fold.'

As the constant corner-by-corner pro-

gramming becomes more automatic, so the lap speeds become more realistic. Every lap is timed, though none is released until *after* the Sunday race. 'I would ask you not to measure yourself against your course colleagues', says Kirkpatrick, although he inevitably has to repeat himself throughout the week. 'The baseline between you is not going to be the same. The capability to sort out potential trouble is not going to be the same. But the Golden Rule is the same, and that's never stick your neck out. Lap consistently, show us that your control of the situation is such that you can actually stick to the rev limits. Consistent improvements alone show us that you know what the hell you're doing out there.'

Sometimes, especially early on in the course, you'll wonder whether you do know what you're doing. Later, with more skid circuit experience in Alfa Romeo saloons and a few illuminating laps in an old Formula Ford Lotus 51, you'll feel much happier. A few solid days of driving and talking and drinking nothing but the dips and turns and landmarks of Snetterton help considerably. Then, you'll begin to believe that you do indeed know what you are doing — and that's the potentially dangerous stage. Confidence threatens to surpass experience, and it immediately shows. The laps in the Esso liveried Van Diemen RF78s become a little quicker, their conduct a lot more rushed. Tyres begin to squeal at new points on the circuit, and the previously artificial braking points can no longer be ignored. Miss the turning-in point, and you will indeed exit wide. Exit wide, and you'll exit slowly. Exit slowly on Sunday, and half your fellow students will come charging past. The Jim Russell school end-of-course race is not only a tremendous experience in itself, but also a powerful stimulus throughout the week. Motivation, like the extremely high standard of tuition at the JRRDS, counts for a lot.

Contrary to possible belief, that tuition is not entirely limited to the classroom. Beyond the initial but important introductory talk, Kirkpatrick, Paine and Co. teach intensively to a queue of drivers-and-cars between the six-lap driving sessions. These sessions begin at 3,500 rpm, after a confidence-boosting straightline acclimatization run. After more than 100 laps and as many critical remarks, 5,500 rpm is reached. To the outsider, it might look rather tame. To the insiders — 12 guys who had never sat in a racing car until a few days previously — 115 mph on the back straight is agreed to be quite sufficient. It is the precision, not the pace, that they are trained to take pride in. With one, the other should follow.

At the course's conclusion, the released lap times endorse this philosophy. Laps completed

Kirkpatrick again, pointing out advice to a worried rookie who looks suspiciously like the author. Personal — and ruthless — criticism is an important feature between six-lap driving stints at the Jim Russell establishment.

Nervous anticipation: after a week of intensive training, 12 young men previously unaccustomed to racing cars are 'thrown in at the deep end'. The Jim Russell School is bravely prepared to show the public that it has 'taught them to swim' — it's an open race meeting, and the pupils are first on the programme!

The race itself provides an exhilarating climax to the Jim Russell Eight-Day course. Surrounded by nervous tutors, Aussie military pilot Steve Byrnes lines up alongside pole position man Bingham!

But to the victor go the spoils... and in this case, the victor under Jim Russell rules was fifth on the road. Unlike the four drivers in front of him, South African student Paddy Flynn did not miss a gear, and did not consequently exceed the imposed 5,500 rpm limit! The winner of his first race is interviewed by Snetterton commentator Norman Greenway and the omnipresent Mr Russell. Like so many others before him, this student travelled half-way across the globe for the course, 'but wouldn't have missed it for the world!'

Instruction on the specially constructed Skid Circuit at Snetterton forms a substantial part of Jim Russell courses. Witness the amount of time pupils spend travelling backwards, and it is easy to understand why.

clumsily within 135 seconds have become laps conducted smoothly some 45 seconds quicker. The competence of those in the JRRDS race was such that even world weary marshals felt moved to applaud. Despite the excitement of race conditions, there were no banged wheels, no wild off course excursions, and just one tail-end spinner. There was also a widespread sense of achievement, of relief, possibly even of disbelief. Just one week earlier, such a performance would have seemed unimaginable. That in itself is justification of the course: a week in which you will find your race driving surprisingly bad, only to make some equally surprising improvements. Opinion amongst 'Old Boys' is as unanimous as farewells are sad: everyone learns a lot, and enjoys themselves even more. Some even talk about buying a Formula Ford...

RACING SCHOOLS AT A GLANCE

	PEACOCK	JIM RUSSELL	TAYLOR
Address	Peacock International Racing Drivers' Schools, South Street, Caerwys, Nr. Mold, Clwyd CH7 5AL Tel: (0352) 720398	Jim Russell International Racing Drivers School, London Road, Downham Market, Norfolk PE38 0DF Tel: (0366) 383397	Ian Taylor Racing Drivers School, Kiln Meadow, Oare, Hermitage, Berks Tel: (0635) 200205
Contact	Richard Peacock or Rosemary Crosslé	Managing Director, John Paine	Managing Director, Ian Taylor
Circuit(s) used	Aintree, nr. Liverpool (1.64 miles) Kirkistown, N. Ireland (1.53 miles)	Snetterton, nr. Norwich (1.92 miles)	Thruxton, nr. Andover (2.36 miles)
Frequency of courses	Once per week average	One per week in season Six Eight-Day courses per year	10 days each month in season
Cars used	FF1600 Crosslé 32Fs Ford Escort	FF1600 Van Diemen RF78s	FF1600 Tigas, Sports 2000 Tiga, FF1600 Taylor Trainer; Lancia Beta Coupé on Open Days
Instructors	Richard Peacock: club racer since 1969, full-time involvement since 1975	John Kirkpatrick: widely respected instructor for 12 years, former sports car racer. John Paine: MD and former Formula Junior racer	Ian Taylor: former British F3 Champion. James Weaver: FF Champion, professional driver. Andrew Gilbert-Scott: F3 frontrunner. Marcus Pye: journalist and regular track tester. Bill Coombs, Grey Headley, Jeremy Lord. Guest appearances by Stirling Moss
Year of establishment	1978	1957	1981
Minimum age of students	Not answered	17	None
Driving Licence necessary?	Yes	No	No
Cost of a trial lesson	£35	£37.50	£45
Cost of a full course	£545 for 10 stages	£645 for Eight Day course	£390
Maximum rpm allowed in last stage	5,700 rpm	5,500 rpm	5,500 rpm
Is skid pan training included?	No	Yes	No
What qualities are sought in instructors?	Ability to make instruction interesting and enjoyable	Ability to communicate well, to adapt to individuals, to analyse driving faults	Race experience and the ability to teach
The school's most successful 'graduates'	John 'Butcher' Booth Ken Gough David Mellor Andy Middlehurst	Emerson Fittipaldi Derek Bell Roberto Guerrero Danny Sullivan	School still too new
Additional notes		Eight day course includes school race. Credit terms available over 12 months.	

Continued on following page

RACING SCHOOLS AT A GLANCE (CONT.)

	SILVERSTONE	TOURACO	BRANDS HATCH
Address	Silverstone Racing School, Unit 22, Silverstone Circuit, Towcester, Northants NN12 8TL Tel: (0327) 857177	Team Touraco International Racing Drivers School, Unit 7, Northolme Industrial Estate, Louth, Lincs Tel: (0507) 601726	Brands Hatch Racing, Brands Hatch Circuit Ltd, Fawkham, Dartford, Kent Tel: (0474) 872331
Contact	Manager, Gerry Corbett or Assistant Manager, Derek Smith	Managing Director, Graeme Glew	Penny Wilson or Fiona Webb
Circuit(s) used	Silverstone, nr. Towcester (1.61 miles, Club circuit)	Cadwell Park, nr. Louth (2.25 miles)	Brands Hatch, nr. Fawkham (1.20 miles, Club circuit)
Frequency of courses	Two days per week in season	Three days per week, for 10 months of the year	Two days per week
Cars used	FF1600 Van Diemens MG Maestros for saloon course	FF1600 Lola T540 and Crosslés BMW 320, Fiesta 1.6	FF1600 Royales Ford Escort XR3s
Instructors	Gerry Corbett: an instructor for 12 years. Derek Smith: an instructor in FF for 5 years	Graeme Glew: raced FF from 1977 to 1980. Robin Parsons: Ford Fiesta frontrunner and FF racer	Tony Lanfranchi: widely experienced and still a saloon car winner. Others in assistance
Year of establishment	1984	1979	—
Minimum age of students	None	17	None
Driving licence necessary?	No	No	No
Cost of a trial lesson	£35	£25	£50
Cost of a full course	£500 FF1600s £405 Saloons	£475 including accommodation	£605
Maximum rpm allowed in last stage	6,000 rpm	6,000 rpm	—
Is skid pan training included?	No	No	Can be arranged
What qualities are sought in instructors?	The skill to control & communicate with pupils, whatever their personal ability and status	Friendliness and personal approach	—
The school's most successful 'graduates'	School still too new	Mark Peters Mark Newby Peter Hardman	—
Additional notes	New in '84, taking over from previous Jim Russell lease with same staff	Very helpful beyond initial schooling, offering cost price car hire to 12 best students each year. 6 then share Team Touraco regular FF1600	Best known for introducing public at large to racing cars. Gaps above due to incomplete questionnaire answers

5 Formula Ford 2000

Like its smaller 1600 cc counterpart, Formula Ford 2000 has flourished. And although FF2000 may not yet be of quite the same interest to readers of this book as FF1600, its place in motor racing does at least warrant description. It is a place of increasing competitiveness and economic attraction; a place within relatively easy reach of all those who have either achieved their desired success in FF1600, or who have simply tired of the formula. To aspiring World Champions and hobby racers alike, FF2000 makes very good sense.

Because it was launched as recently as 1975, FF2000 is still visibly evolving. After a rather hesitant first season, the formula was widely dismissed for several more years as little more than a wealthy businessman's play thing. It was almost a category that provided single-seater racing for those who liked 'real' racing cars, but liked rather less the kamikaze tactics of embryonic superstars.

In the decade since, FF2000's credibility has snowballed: it has attracted a greater number of 'serious' drivers, more respect, and yet more serious career drivers. Not least, FF2000 can now offer a useful stepping-stone in the middle of the vast financial gulf between FF1600 and F3. Consider that, even at its most costly, a top team drive in FF1600 might cost £40,000, and that an equivalent seat in Formula Three would cost £100,000 or more. And then consider that FF2000 front runners can manage with a budget of £40,000. It can easily be seen why some experts predict that FF2000 will one day actually replace Formula Three.

When devised in the mid 1970s, Formula Ford 2000 was intended not only as a logical progression from FF1600, but also a technically easy one. Competitors wishing to make the move could retain their existing FF1600 chassis and simply bolt on the different bodywork, racing slicks in place of treaded tyres, and of course the bigger engine. A new monocoque itself was not needed.

A decade later, the essential difference between FF1600 and 2000 remains unchanged. Although it is not very often that a driver will actually bolt-on an FF2000 conversion, it is increasingly likely that he will consider the move up to FF2000. Whilst the slipping and sliding 1600 cc cars teach the raw art of car control and racing in traffic, the two-litre Ford formula introduces the learning driver to slightly more power, significantly more grip and downforce, and many more considerations when setting a car up to suit particular circuit conditions. In other words, it cultivates the necessary ability to think beyond the innate natural reflexes that can win races in FF1600.

FF2000's changing role is reflected in the changing character of its participants (who, incidentally, must have an international racing licence, which is obtainable after acceptable behaviour in six 'restricted' races in FF1600). Unquestionably the most famous success story to have emerged from a spell in FF2000 is that of Ayrton Senna. The exceptionally talented Brazilian was a Rushen Green Racing Van Diemen FF2000 driver in 1982 — and a Toleman seated Grand Prix regular by 1984. Like his compatriot Emerson Fittipaldi, he showed vividly just how winning in Formula Ford can further a driver's career. By winning in Formula Three, he was able to prove that his previous success in FF2000 had actually meant something. It increasingly does.

During his FF2000 season, Senna won both

For many years, FF2000 attracted drivers who raced purely for enjoyment, such as Mike 'Fulmar' Taylor seen here at the Nürburgring. This shot shows the printing company director in his 1983 Reynard – by 1984, he had switched to Sports 2000. The reason, he said, was that 'FF2000 is now simply too expensive to be treated only as a hobby. It's a terrific formula, it's quite tough, but it's become another place for aspiring World Champions'.

Brazilian Ayrton Senna underlined the value of FF2000 as a step on the ladder to stardom in 1982 – by 1984, he had a regular drive in Grands Prix.

Power oversteer, illustrated by 1983 British FF2000 Champion, Tim Davies.

the British and European Championships. His only serious adversary, and runner-up in both series, was Norfolkman Calvin Fish, whose participation in FF2000 tells its own interesting tale. As a regular winner in Superkarts, with their almost rigid suspension and aerodynamic wings and startling 150 mph capability, Fish was unable to raise much enthusiasm for FF1600. In comparison, he said, their suspension was soggy, their squealing and sliding tyres tedious, the general driving style ragged. But FF2000 was different: racing tyres, adjustable wings, the need for more precise driving. 'It was', he says succinctly, 'more like driving a *real* racing car. Formula Ford 2000 is an excellent grounding for any driver wishing to go on to Formula Three, and possibly higher.'

Inevitably, the two-litre, Pinto engined formula also has its disadvantages. Increasing competitiveness means increasing costs, and decreasing practicability to the driver simply seeking Sunday fun. And more seriously, in the early 1980s, tyres alone have sometimes literally made the difference between winning and losing. Because the tyres vary in both adhesion and durability, some sets can prove significantly better than others. The larger a driver's choice, the greater his possibility of finding a tyre advantage — and, ultimately, the greater the formula's costs.

'When I was in FF2000', recalls Fish, 'we found that there was an enormous amount of time to be gained from just the tyres. If you can afford

to, have several sets of wheels, and go out and test methodically with all your tyres to find the good sets. You can spend a hundred laps trying to alter the car to improve your lap time by a couple-of-tenths, and yet you can sometimes find half-a-second just by changing the tyres, just like that! It's obviously not an ideal situation, and it can't be good for the formula, but it's there at the moment and you have to tackle it.'

Senna's former FF Team Manager, Snetterton based Dennis Rushen, confirms this FF2000 quirk. 'People got upset with us when we were running Ayrton in 'two-litre', he admits, 'and accused us of all sorts of things on the subject of tyres. But we just spent all our time sorting out tyres rather than sorting out the car. If we got understeer, we'd change the front tyres; if we got oversteer, we'd change the rear tyres. We'd sometimes stand there in the pit lane with five or six complete sets of tyres stacked up around us. It is almost an unfair advantage if you've got the budget to do this. There were times when it even flattered Senna, when he was winning by seventeen or more seconds — we all know he's very good, but no-one's *that* good.'

A depressing prospect, perhaps, but it must be hoped that by the time you read this the Powers That Be will have solved the unhappy problem. And it can only be said that Senna's rocketing progress through the motor racing ranks has powerfully illustrated the many advantages of FF2000.

Formula Ford 2000's new, slimline look. This is the 1984 works Van Diemen of Irishman Martin Donnelly. Though it looked good, at the time of writing it was struggling to keep up with the FF2000 Reynards.

The difference between FF1600 and FF2000, in this case 1984 Reynards. Wider tyres and aerodynamic wings distinguish the two-litre car.

Yes, FF2000 racing can be exciting!

At the 'hobby' level — but nonetheless also very competitive — is long-time FF2000 contender and frequent race winner, Mike 'Fulmar' Taylor. The director of Fulmar Colour Printing races purely for enjoyment, but does so very seriously. He has also raced in both FF1600 and Sports 2000, and has concluded that FF2000 has a greater attraction. 'In 1600', he confesses with a chuckle, 'you get to the point where you *feel* old, even though you're only 28 or 29. You've got budding stars racing with you who are not much more than half your age, and there's the pressure of the factory works team as well. In FF2000, even in a non-works team, you can go out there knowing that the racing's going to be as tough, but that there are less favoured drivers with a possible technical advantage: the competition is fierce, but possibly more fair.

'Having done Sports 2000 for a year, though, I think it put FF2000 nicely into perspective. In the sports cars, you just wander onto the track and do your best, but by comparison FF2000 is like lemmings jumping off the edge of a cliff! That extra edge in the competition makes all the difference, and it means there's a lot of kudos in being a successful FF2000 driver — you can consider that if you're competitive in FF2000, you could probably be competitive in anything. Like FF1600, it actually counts for something, but maybe ultimately more so, because you're having to race with your brain as well as your balls!

'In Formula Ford 2000, there are a lot of cars out there, and a lot of overtaking. In Formula Three, how often do the positions change during a race? You only have to look at Ayrton Senna, one of the most talented young drivers in a long time: when he wanted to overtake Martin Brundle in F3, he either got stuck behind him, or crashed. FF2000 isn't like that. It's real racing cars *and* real racing.'

6 Setting-up and driving technique

During the early 1980s, Mark Peters emerged as one of Britain's brightest hopes for future racing stardom. Successful on the track, he is thoughtful and articulate off it. In what is too often considered a rough and tumble 'brawn' formula, Peters' approach emphasises the importance of 'brain'.

Mark was the winner of the BARC Junior Championship in 1981, when he missed making it a championship double, in the Dunlop/ Autosport Star of Tomorrow series, by just 0.02 seconds! He endured a less rewarding season in 1982, winning races only after switching marques mid-stream in dissatisfaction. By 1983 Peters had reiterated his promise, finishing a serious runner-up to the highly acclaimed Andrew Gilbert-Scott in the top Townsend Thoresen series. As an appointed member of the works Van Diemen FF1600 team, he has also won much respect as a shrewd test and development driver. Here, Mark explains some important points in the approach to driving, and advises on the vital ways of really getting the most from your car...

Nowadays, Formula Ford 1600 is a highly specialised and technical business. The modern-day FF1600 car is a sophisticated machine, which requires setting-up properly to cope with the many variables presented by motor racing. In most cases, it is best to have a knowledgeable mechanic working on your car for you. Even though a typical Formula Ford driver's style is ragged, his car still has to be set-up precisely. Getting it right is very important.

Perhaps the most important aspect of setting a car is roll bar adjustment. Only a slight alteration to a roll bar setting can bring about a substantial change in a car's handling characteristics.

Basically, stiffening a front roll bar will promote understeer, stiffening the rear will induce oversteer. A new car will usually arrive from a manufacturer with both bars set mid-way through their adjustment range. The inherent tendency of an FF1600 chassis is to oversteer, whether the rear roll bar is set particularly soft or stiff. Increased stiffness, however, will make the oversteer more predictable, and make the chassis more responsive — consequently, it will be easier to drive quickly.

Mark Peters.

Dramatic oversteer and one front wheel off the deck, our chapter writer Mark Peters makes a rare mistake that his pursuer, Andrew Gilbert-Scott, is able to take advantage of.

A Formula Ford car will spend a great deal of time sliding around, and a driver should aim to find a happy medium between throwing his car into a corner, and applying the power smoothly once he is in it. He should try to slide his car without actually scrubbing off any speed. There is no point entering a corner too quickly, and braking too late — that just loses time. Seek to achieve a smooth, fluid driving motion. Roll bar adjustment is an easy and effective way of altering a car's behaviour to suit a particular circuit, or set of conditions. In the wet, for example, a car should have a soft roll bar at the front, although not fully soft, and a fully soft one at the rear.

Many people think that it is wise to disconnect a rear roll bar completely in the wet. This is not so. It may improve rear end grip to a degree, but it also brings about snap oversteer. Once the car starts to spin, it becomes very hard to stop it when the rear bar is disconnected, and it is therefore best to leave it connected.

Take things gently, and make small changes one step at a time. That way, purely through trial and error, you should safely be able to find the most suitable roll bar requirements for a given set of circumstances.

Once acceptable roll bar settings have been found, there are a further three essential items to consider: ride heights, camber, and spring ratings.

Firstly, ride heights. Lowering a car can improve the position of its centre of gravity, and therefore diminish body roll and increase grip. Ideally, a car should be able to circulate set as low as possible, without reaching a point where it is bottoming on the track. Obviously, ride heights will have to be altered to suit different circuits, and also to compensate for drivers of different weights. Again, take things one step at a time, and work towards the correct set-up without making excessive alterations. Sudden, drastic, changes in a car's behaviour can easily catch people out — and accidents can be rather expensive to repair.

One point to remember is that the lower a car becomes, so the more its wheel camber will increase, putting pressure on a different area of the tyres. To maintain the equlibrium, reduce camber as you reduce the ride height. When the car begins to bottom, stop, and move the ride heights up one notch. That should produce the optimum centre of gravity.

It is always worth fitting steel or aluminium 'skids' to the underside of a car. In the event of bottoming, these will wear away, but they are much cheaper to replace than a wrinkled floorpan.

As for the camber of the wheels, it is essential to keep a close check on tyre wear. A surplus of tread on the outside of a tyre, when there is comparatively little on the inside, is

69

indicative of too much camber. If the situation is reversed, with a dearth of tread on the outside and plenty inside, then a car is running with insufficient camber. A camber gauge can be used to reset a car to its recommended settings, which will be available from the manufacturer, whatever its vintage.

If a car is oversteering too much, then an increase in camber should offer more grip. By making continual, small adjustments, a driver can soon find an acceptable balance. It is crucial to make small changes, principally because it is very easy to go over the top and change the car's feel entirely. And remember, whenever a camber change is effected, the tyres will wear differently. Always run the car for a few laps to heat the tyres properly in their new position. You won't learn much about how the car may have changed until the tyres are properly bedded in. Camber basically effects and changes a car's level of grip. Although most changes are likely to centre around the rear, driving wheels, changes to the front can also be considered, to improve front end grip when turning into slow corners.

Finally, there are springs to consider. These are available with many different poundage ratings. Essentially, differently rated springs will alter a car much as a roll bar adjustment will,

increasing the softness or stiffness of a chassis as required. If a set of springs is too hard, the car may begin to bounce off kerbs. If too soft, the car may well stand on its nose under braking.

Springs of different ratings are worth experimenting with, and a driver can usually ascertain by instinct exactly which set suits his equipment best. Changing springs is rather more expensive than effecting a simple roll bar adjustment, however, and so the latter will be more important to a beginner.

It is more difficult to appreciate the difference new springs have made until you have done a considerable mileage with them fitted. The main benefits of spring alterations are likely to be found in improved braking, and increased traction out of slow corners.

Gleaning information about roll bar settings, ride height adjustments, cambers and spring ratings will of course require a driver to do some testing mileage. The cost of a day, or even half-a-day, testing will always be money well spent for a beginner. Acclimatizing to a car will obviously be useful, while, providing you are sensible, continual experimenting can be both educational and practical.

When trying to sort out your car, remember that you are basically aiming to achieve the most

A classic case of controlled oversteer, and an inevitable fast driver's Formula Ford poise, exhibited by Brazilian Maurizio Sandro Sala.

neutral handling characteristics that you can. A well-balanced car will prove to be easier to drive, and will enable the fastest lap times to be recorded. Effecting subtle alterations will also teach a driver how to adjust a chassis to his own needs, which will stand him in good stead should he progress in the sport.

There are other matters, out of the cockpit, which should also be considered in an effort to improve your racing car. Most Formula Ford manufacturers, for instance, run 'works' teams. By keeping in touch with the manufacturer, you can often pick up hints gained through the racing experience of others, which may well prove beneficial. Such information may save on testing time, and also reduce expense. Racing cars, like clothing, have to be tailored to suit the individual, and the more information you can pick up, the more likely you are to be able to fit a car to your own requirements.

It is important to experiment, principally to find the limits of any new settings. If you should find that your car is oversteering, for example, then there is no point just rushing in to the pits and changing everything in sight. Make changes by degrees. Concentrate upon making one alteration at a time to either the front or the rear of the car, as required. See what sort of effect that particular change produces before you venture onto anything else.

A growing library of information can be of ever-increasing use as you become more familiar with your car, and to this end it is a good idea to make a note of everything you learn at each test session. This can prove to be very useful whenever you return to any particular circuit for an actual race.

If you are due to race at Brands Hatch one weekend, for example, then it is obviously a good idea to undertake a test session there during the preceding week. Other circuits may prove to be more convenient, however, and it is always worth bearing in mind that a circuit such as Snetterton can be of tremendous use for testing purposes. Blessed with a wide variety of types of corner, it can assist greatly in familiarisation with your car.

Wherever you happen to be testing, it is a good idea to make a note of lap times, and the number of revs you are pulling on the exit of a corner, or at a given point on a straight. Try and

And the other extreme, shown by Geoff Lees' Royale.

Same corner, same day, same formula – but different ideas of 'the limit'! James Weaver shows how it should be done at the Snetterton Esses...

...but a rival shows how it shouldn't. The most spectacular way is not always the most effective...

... as these two gentlemen surely illustrate.

find out how many revs other drivers are pulling at the same points, and if they are faster than you, concentrate upon improving your technique at that part of the circuit until you are capable of maintaining a consistently high speed. Try to do the same for any corner around which you feel you are particularly slow. Keeping a record of the rpm at specific points will furnish you with a direct target to aim at on your next visit — a target you should subsequently try to beat.

In addition to the ways in which you can change a car's handling already discussed, there are a few tips other than effecting roll bar adjustments which ought to be borne in mind for

73

wet conditions. Above all else, it is essential to be smooth in the wet. Apply power smoothly, and try to avoid excessive wheelspin and loss of traction. The rain demands a very different driving technique, for which it is usually best to adjust a car's brake balance bias to the rear – quite extensively so. It is also advisable to increase tyre pressures by between two and four pounds. This opens up the tyre's grooves slightly, affording increased grip.

Whilst roll bar settings and tyres can be experimented with in the wet, it is equally imperative to work upon perfecting your driving technique. And you can always learn to make the most of the conditions. Look out for the driest stretches of tarmac around corners, and avoid puddles. Even if that means straying from the usual recommended racing line, the better traction will save time. Gear ratios, too, should be changed in the wet. A 'lower' set of ratios will suit the inevitably slower speeds everywhere.

Whether it is wet or dry, it is wise to practice your starting technique during a test day, provided that the track is clear, of course. The start of any race is important, but this is especially so in Formula Ford, where competitors are, on paper, fairly evenly matched. A good start can produce a

useful advantage over a rival for the early stages of a race.

Ideally, you should aim to have the clutch just at its biting point, while holding the engine somewhere between 5,000 and 5,500 rpm, blipping the throttle gently. Naturally, you want to be delicately balanced so that the clutch can be released the moment the lights turn to green. In the wet, smoothness again becomes imperative, and you should attempt to leave the line almost as though you were driving a road car.

The complete novice can save a lot of accident repair bills by observing some of the most important, yet nonetheless overlooked, codes of practice. Mirrors are frequently a stumbling block, and these should be kept properly adjusted at all times to ensure maximum rearward vision. Racing harnesses should be kept tight, as it is much easier to fully appreciate the feel of the car if you are securely strapped in. Once you are comfortably ensconced, the pedals and the gear linkage can always be altered to suit individual needs.

Such things may appear trivial at first, but careful presentation should make for a safer progression.

When you are first starting, try to find a

Furthest from the camera, Mark Peters makes a good start. It is easier said than done – do not be ashamed to practice.

Do not become completely demoralised if practice is needed in abundance. Even the best make mistakes!

sensible compromise. You don't want to reach the first corner too quickly and disappear irretrievably into the barriers; nor do you want to be too slow, and find the corners too easy. Begin steadily and progress at a cautious rate.

Before even thinking about venturing out onto the track, wait until the engine has had a chance to warm up for a few minutes. The water temperature should reach about 50°C before you set off. Once you are on the track, allow some time for the gearbox oil and tyres to reach optimum working temperatures. If you take things steadily to begin with, and temper with a little common sense any over-eagerness to progress, then you will leave the circuit at the end of the day with your car still in one piece, other drivers permitting.

You will soon pick up all sorts of useful information. For example, smearing a thin layer of washing up liquid on the inside of your crash helmet visor prevents the usual problem of steaming-up in the wet. When sitting in the midst of a gridful of cars on a rainy day, it might come in quite handy to see the start lights come on! Be meticulous in your approach, and observe what the more experienced competitors are up to. Never be afraid to ask advice.

Make sure that you can settle yourself into your car comfortably. The more comfortable you are, the more confident you will feel. Make sure that your overalls aren't too tight when you sit down...an obvious point, but one that is easy to overlook.

The essential thing about preparing yourself for racing is care. A well thought out approach to the sport is far more likely to produce dividends than a rushed one. Patience and willingness to learn will serve you well in the long run.

Common sense will also prove to be a useful asset in a race. A driver should use his brain, and not rush into making rash manoeuvres. If you find yourself amid a pack of dicing FF1600 cars, always assume that the driver ahead hasn't seen you. And plan your overtaking manoeuvres with that in mind. Allow for sudden movements from your nearest rival, too – it will be entirely possible that he hasn't seen you lurking just behind him.

The main point is, don't rush things. It's often worth spending a lap behind a driver that you hope to overtake, to look out for the future overtaking possibilities. See if you can spot where you are quicker than he is, and see whether or not it would make a suitable point at which to mount a challenge. Don't try to rush by at every corner,

75

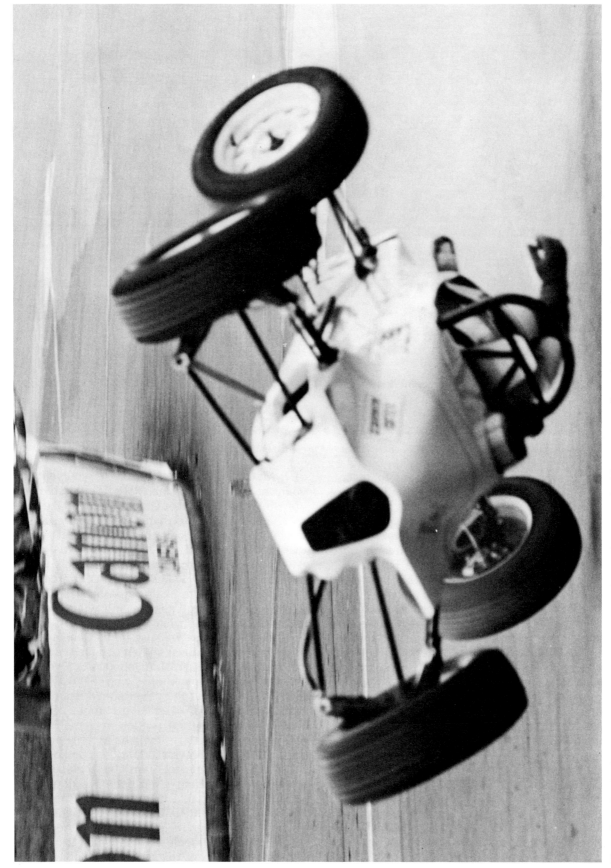

There is an instinctive temptation during accidents to 'protect' your head with your arms. Once things start going dramatically wrong, try to keep yourself tucked into the cockpit. This is Miguel-Angel Lopez at Silverstone's Woodcote chicane, losing the battle against centrifugal force.

and if you have to follow him for a few laps, don't keep repeating the same manoeuvres — he'll soon get wise to that.

Use your brain! Out-thinking somebody frequently has more effect than outbraking somebody. If you know that you can get past a rival, don't be foolhardy, but wait until you can seize a safe opportunity to squeeze ahead. By charging into an overtaking attempt, you will only increase your chances of having an accident, and that will neither win you friends nor do your career any favours.

On the track, the worst lap is often the first one. Inevitably the most crowded time of the race, it is also usually the most precarious, with all of the world and his dog trying to outsmart each other. Stay calm, and appraise the situation. If you can keep clear of trouble, you will still be in the running to mount a challenge at the end.

Even in the busiest races, don't forget to pay close attention to the marshals' flag signals. Do your homework properly, and learn to respond automatically to all the signals. Failure to obey a flag instruction is almost certain to lead to your disqualification from the results, and that won't be easy to explain to the sponsors.

To master fully the art of racecraft, it is really necessary to gain first hand experience of racing conditions. However, test sessions can be of great help, particularly in assisting a driver to sort out his braking points and general technique. Conditions may vary in a race, of course, and the best line through a corner won't always be available. All the same, it is important to work on being smooth.

If you brake, or accelerate, in the middle of a bend, you will cause weight transfer, and upset a car's balance. Always brake in a straight line, before you turn in. Keep an eye out for conspicuous land marks: advertising hoardings, marshals' posts and the like. Remember that marshals themselves, or photographers, are prone to move, throwing your system into disarray. Make a mental note of where you are braking, and leave it a little later each time, as you progress, until you reach a point where you are able to complete a smooth sequence of braking and down-changing to the optimum turn-in point.

To get some idea of where you should be apexing, there are several tell-tale signs to look out for. If a particular part of the kerbing is covered in tyre marks, or has been worn away or perhaps recently renewed, it is a sure indication of the clipping point. Work hard at your consistency

and accuracy, and the benefit of such application to technique will soon be revealed by the stopwatch.

There are also several other little, but important, things that a driver ought to acclimatise himself to. One of these is the right-hand gearchange found in a Formula Ford car. That will come very naturally, but you must concentrate on making changes as fast and smooth as possible. FF1600 gearboxes are usually quite strong!

Always scrub your tyres in before a race, and never try to compete on brand new rubber. A car will feel very skittish on new tyres, so keep an eye on your lap times. When the times come down, it is a sign that the tyres are ready.

One fairly fundamental point to consider is the amount of petrol that you put in the car before a race. Putting in too much can be as much a disadvantage as putting in too little. Also, keep a regular check on your car's weight. Ensure that it remains within the prescribed limits. If a car is too heavy, consult its manufacturer, who will be able to suggest ways of paring off the surplus.

Still on the subject of weight, cornerweights on an FF1600 car can affect braking performance quite significantly. These, too, are best checked closely at regular intervals. If you don't have access to a cornerweight gauge, a manufacturer should always be able to assist with information.

Two concluding points. First, it's often worth re-examining a car's ride height when it's at operating temperature, to allow for the possible expansion of any metal joints once the car has warmed up. Secondly, if you find yourself getting into trouble in a race, always keep as much of your body in the car as you can. When overturning, many drivers are tempted to try and shield their heads with their hands. A crash helmet will provide the best protection available to your head. All you will be doing in such a situation is also putting your arms at risk.

That, as with any racing situation, really just requires the application of a little common sense. Pay attention to detail and work hard towards achieving any motor racing goals that you have set yourself; you will need to use your brain as much as you will need to be brave. The car won't help you in any way, so it is up to you entirely to channel your attentions into building up a compendium of practical information, related to all aspects of racing driving. Take everything a step at a time, and you will at least give yourself a chance of success.

7 The top ten circuits

The principles of driving a Formula Ford car to best effect are one thing. The specifics of racing driving, which vary from circuit to circuit, are of course another. And the circuits themselves vary enormously too. What follows is a look at the top ten tracks used regularly by Formula Fords in Britain, with succinct analysis again from Mark Peters...

Brand Hatch Grand Prix
This full circuit is only available one day each year for testing, and that's a day to make the most of. Gear-wise, the requirements are: third for Paddock, which is the dramatic downhill turn after the pits, then second for Druids, third for Graham Hill bend, second for Surtees, then up into top along the Pilgrims Drop straight. A good exit speed from Surtees, pulling high revs, is essential. The next corner, Hawthorns, can be taken flat in top, and this can make the difference between a fast lap and an indifferent one. Westfield and Dingle Dell should be taken in third, whilst the tighter Stirlings merits second. This leads you back onto the Indy circuit, and onto Clearways, which requires third. Then it's into top over the start/finish line, and off you go again.

Brands Hatch Indy
The shorter of Brands' two car racing circuits revolves around Clearways, at least as far as setting a fast lap is concerned. Paddock, Druids, and Graham Hill are all taken the same way as they would be on the Grand Prix circuit. Turn into Surtees in second, and hold it until you reach the exit of Clearways, where you select third. A fast, clean exit here can be worth a lot of time.

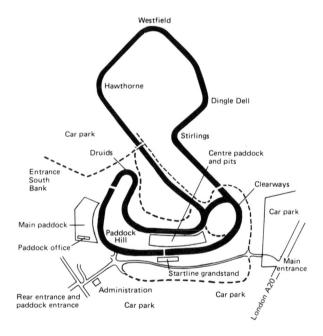

BRANDS HATCH

On both the Club and Grand Prix circuits, Paddock Bend is one of the most difficult corners at Brands Hatch. During the opening laps, there can be a wide diversity of lines...

...but the corner does have its limitations.

Silverstone Grand Prix

A very fast circuit, this one, which can depend upon speed through two corners in particular, Stowe and Club. Before that, Copse is a third gear right, leading to Maggotts, which is a flat-in-top kink when it is dry. A quick downchange to second is needed for Becketts, out of which you grab third for Chapel, and fourth as you come onto Hangar Straight. Stowe and Club come next, and these two very fast right handers can be taken in either third or top, depending upon gear ratios and prevailing winds. Too sideways in either of these bends, and you will lose very valuable seconds.

Out of Club, Abbey is flat in top, and the notorious Woodcote Chicane, for which it is often hard to find a good braking point, is taken in third.

Silverstone Club

Silverstone's club circuit has just three corners, the Copse being the only one common to both Club and GP tracks. On the club circuit, you find that Becketts is a tight, second-gear hairpin, out of which you must pull a high number of revs for the following Club Straight. At the end of the straight, Woodcote is a tightening right-hander, necessitating third gear.

On either of Silverstone's circuits, you will find slipstreaming is the order of the day. Work at this, and always try to plan ahead, remembering that it is best to slipstream past a rival just before the braking point for a corner.

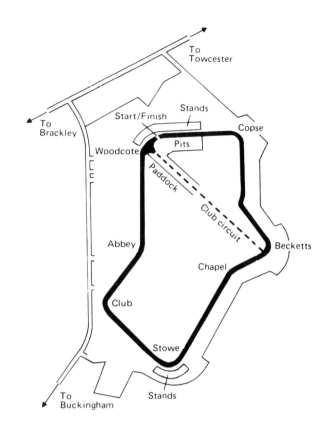

SILVERSTONE

The Woodcote Chicane on the Silverstone GP circuit demands speed with precision. Overtaking in the braking area is where races can be won or lost in the last lap race for the line. (Here, Renault Grand Prix driver Derek Warwick hustles his Hawke around the kerbing in front of Bernard Devaney).

On the short circuit, Woodcote becomes a tight but crucial right-hander that leads onto the pits straight. Again, overtaking under braking is common, but so, too, are mistakes. Gianfranco Cané's works Van Diemen and Jim Walsh's Royale suffer a misunderstanding.

Donington Park

Donington's track surface can be a problem in the wet, because kerosene deposits from low-flying aircraft in the vicinity can combine with rain to form a lethal mixture. (The circuit is near the East Midlands Airport).

That aside, Redgate requires third gear, and a late turning-in point. A car shouldn't be thrown in to the corner, as a smooth passage is needed in order to make the most of the stretch between Hollywood and the Old Hairpin, via the swooping Craner Curves. Hollywood and the Curves are taken in top, with third being selected for the Old Hairpin. Good revs are needed on the next exit here, to compensate for the uphill stretch through Starkey's Bridge, and towards McLeans.

The Coppice Wood kink, just after Starkey's Bridge, should be treated almost like a corner: move over to the right of the track and you will emerge straight, on the right trajectory for the braking area into the third gear McLeans. Again, exit speed is crucial for the uphill section into Coppice, a third gear bend with what might be considered as a double apex. Turn in before you see the apex of the corner, and select top as the car comes out onto the long straight leading to the Park Chicane. Enter the chicane slowly, in second gear, and aim to exit as fast as possible for the run up to Redgate.

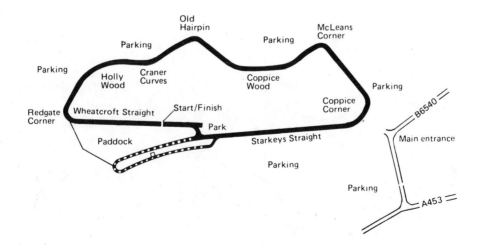

DONINGTON

As many as five-abreast, Formula Fords emerge in the distance from Donington Park's important, double-apex Coppice Corner. The run down Starkeys Straight and under the Dunlop Bridge leads into a tight chicane; again, the braking area is an optimum point for passing manoeuvres.

Another view of Donington, this time at the fast, inclined stretch between the Old Hairpin and Coppice Wood, a quick but deceptive gentle left-hander. With its variety of corners, undulating nature, and open aspect for spectators, Donington is now one of the finest circuits in Europe.

Thruxton

A fast lap on this quick, airfield circuit usually depends on a decent line through the Campbell-Cobb-Segrave complex. Allard, the first corner, should be flat in top, which Thruxton's generous width will easily allow for. You should let your car drift and keep up the engine revs. Keep to the left for the braking area into the complex. Turn in using second gear, and don't take Campbell too quickly. Begin your attack on the lap at Cobb, and then switch up to third as you accelerate out of Campbell. After that, it's flat in top all the way around to the chicane. The left-hander at Kimpton requires an early turn-in point, whilst Goodwood and Church both have conveniently placed marshals' posts, which mark the approximate clipping points.

Beware of the big bump at Church, by the way. The Club Chicane is taken in second, and should be approached from the left of the circuit as you enter the first part. Once clear, select third just before the pedestrian bridge on the start/finish straight, and get into top as quickly as possible for Allard.

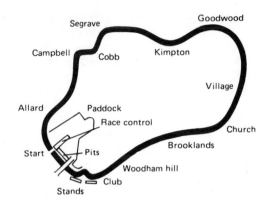

THRUXTON

A marked contrast to Thruxton's very fast sweeps 'out in the country', a tight chicane brings the cars back onto the pits straight in full view of public grandstands. Although it is a slow section of a fast track, a lot of time can be gained – or wasted – here.

Snetterton

Snetterton contains a wide variety of corners, which makes it a good base for testing. The first of these, Riches, can be taken in third or top, depending upon car settings and the wind. It is a double-apex corner, which should allow for plenty of grip. Be careful when exiting Riches, however, as the wind can blow dirt from a neighbouring cabbage field onto the track, and make things a little slippery.

Sears is a tight, 90 degree right, which should be navigated in second. Resist the temptation to use armfuls of oversteer, as a fast exit is essential for the straight leading to the Esses. This is quite a difficult section. Select second under braking before you turn in to the first part, accelerate smoothly in, brake slightly, and then come back on to the power gently for the right-hand exit. You should then be in third gear for the following 'Bomb-hole', really an un-named corner, which is taken flat. Select top before Coram, and hold it in top all the way around, using the inside kerb if necessary. When you've a little experience, you will approach Russell flat in top. This is not recommended for a novice! This can be one of the most dangerous corners in the country, and the biggest mistake is to hit the inside kerbing, which can bounce you into a fairly uncompromising tyre wall. But with practice, this *should* be flat in top!

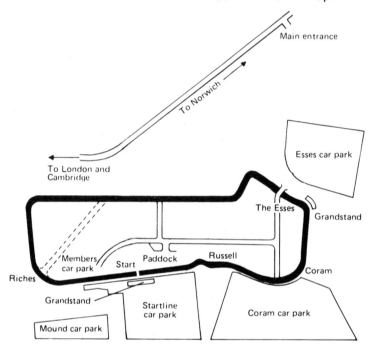

SNETTERTON

First corner bothers at Snetterton's Riches, usually taken by the brave flat in top gear.

Oulton Park

One slight difficulty here is that, at the time of writing, no-one had yet driven competitively around the revised circuit. Of the 'old' corners, Old Hall is a very fast third gear right-hander, which leads down the Avenue towards the 'new' Cascades. You will be in top on the Avenue, and I would estimate that Cascades will require third, the Island Hairpin second, and the rejuvenated Knicker Brook flat in top. It will be interesting to see.

Past Knicker Brook, Druids is a fast, double-apex affair, taken in third, with top being selected on the exit of the corner. Lodge Corner is a tight right, with a fair degree of camber, and needs second gear. Power oversteer can be used to good effect here. Change into third as you leave the dip at the bottom of Lodge, and select top as you crest Deer Leap and come back onto the startline straight.

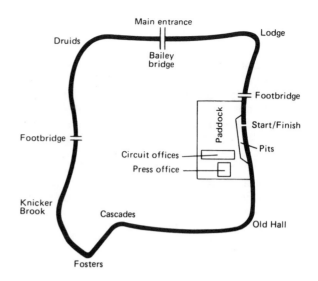

OULTON PARK

The narrow, twisting nature of Oulton Park, lined in parts by very unforgiving railway sleepers. An excellent venue for the encouragement of accuracy!

Cadwell Park

England's 'Mini-Nürburgring', as it is popularly labelled, begins with a fast lefthand kink. This is called Coppice, and is taken in top. The track then moves uphill, and it's into third gear for Charlie's Bend, another quick corner, though this time a right-hander. Grab top again on the exit, and hold it along the straight until you reach the second-gear Park. A tight line can be quite useful here, and it is wise to be smooth in order to be quick into the long right-hander known as Chris Corner, taken in third. Select top as you exit, and prepare for a right-hand kink before The Gooseneck, where you hold top. Mansfield follows, and requires third, then it is back into top until the third gear left which leads into the Mountain. Drop into second gear for the right-hand bend which leads up the Mountain itself, and hold it in second until the Hall Bends, taken in third. Up to the hairpin, and power oversteer can be used in second gear. Upshift to third for Barn, which is a fast, but not flat, right-hander. This takes you back onto the main straight.

One thing: be mindful of the stretch between the hairpin and the aptly named Barn. A farmer crosses the track in his tractor at that point during the week, and the surface occasionally becomes mud-spattered and slippery.

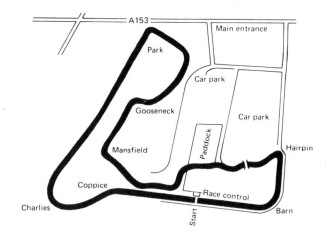

CADWELL PARK

Often described as a mini Nüburgring, Cadwell Park is a twisty and undulating circuit, which demands precision from a driver.

Mallory Park

This is a tight little circuit with only three real corners, and the principal test of speed is at Gerards, a very long, sweeping right-hander. This should be taken in top all the way around, and it can be taken without lifting. It is best, however, to lift slightly from the throttle before you turn in. This will allow you some acceleration around the corner, and consequently a higher exit speed.

The Stebbe Straight will keep you in top all the way to the Lake Esses, taken in third. Hold third all the way up to Shaws Hairpin, which is tight enough to justify using first gear. Enter the corner slowly, and come out quickly, avoiding any excessive use of power oversteer. Snatch second and third gears in quick succession before you swoop down through Devils Elbow, which shouldn't deter you with its sharp camber. Drift wide, very close to the pit lane armco. You then want to be back in top as you cross the startline again, ready for the all-important Gerards.

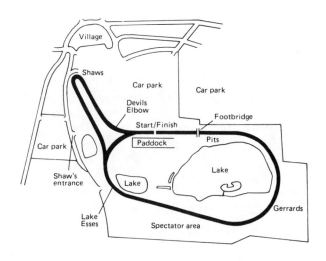

MALLORY PARK

One of the most distinctive corners in the country, Mallory Park's fussy, first-gear hairpin.

Another important bend at Mallory, the fast sweep around the lake, called Gerards.

8 Formula Ford design

H.12373

Even the most intense of Adrian Reynard's rivals will admit that, yes, they can recognise his design genius. They have to, since it is unmistakable. As a result of extensive wind tunnel research, Reynard has recently, and relatively spectacularly, revised the shape of Formula Ford aerodynamics. As a result of a talent that seems as inexhaustible as it does immeasurable, his singular presence has in recent years affected the very nature of Formula Ford racing itself. And neither has his talent been restricted to the drawing board: from the cockpit of his own racing car to the director's desk of his own company, Adrian Reynard has achieved similar success. He says that 'Formula Ford is not only the starting point for all serious racing drivers nowadays, but is an independent industry in its own right.' What he does not need to say is that he is one of its most brilliant industrialists – his results speak loudly enough for themselves.

Although still only in his early thirties, Reynard has turned down the sort of offers many other young designers spend their lives dreaming about. He has remained an influence in Formula Ford not by necessity of his own design or manufacturing limitations, but largely as a reaction to the limitations of others. One of the many things he has learnt in his ten years in motor racing is that he works best as his own boss.

At 29, Reynard was invited to join the design team at Lotus, the envy of any rising British racing car designer. But if he did so, he was told, he would also be obliged to close down his own company, Sabre Automotive. He declined.

At 31, he succumbed to the Formula One temptation and accepted the post of chief engineer at March Grand Prix. But when he did so, he recalls, he soon learnt, 'things weren't done the way I would have done them.' He resigned.

Reynard's resolve is just that: it is difficult to find any trace of arrogance in the man. His is not a strong-headedness, but a strong will. 'Especially after working for myself for ten years', he explains, 'I suppose I realised my future lies with a company in which I control the destiny. I've gone through a steep learning curve in the past few years, and thought it a good time to apply that knowledge to my own company.'

And so he has. Since Adrian won the European FF2000 Championship for himself in 1979, other drivers have gone on to win a further three out of a possible seven valid FF2000 titles for Reynard cars in Britain alone. Abroad, Reynards simply monopolise most markets. It would be easy to attribute such success to Adrian's quite exceptional knowledge, or intelligence, or incisiveness, or imagination. But he says there's also a certain amount of intuition involved in his particular Formula Ford designs.

In the Chapter that he has written here, Adrian Reynard also says some fascinating things about Formula Ford design priorities, about common Formula Ford technical preoccupations such as camber settings, and about crucial matters such as obtaining the most from chassis and tyres together...

When the concept of a new car is born, there follows a period of many months when the designer tries to achieve his ideals on the drawing board. Transferring these ideas into pencil shapes is the first process in a lengthy evolution of a new car. Schemes which may appear practical in the mind often dissolve into unachievable fantasies as they have to be reconciled with the compromises

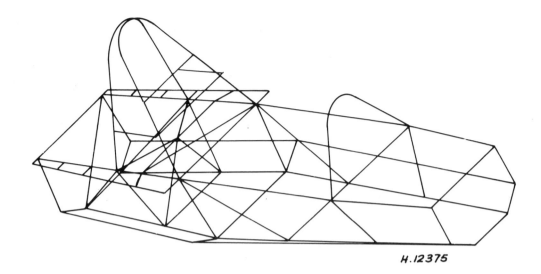

H.12375

Like most other modern technologies, Formula Ford design makes use of the most modern techniques: computer aided graphic design allows a torsionally stiff chassis to be developed with adequate roll over protection, thereby fulfilling two of Reynard's most important design considerations.

necessary in vehicle engineering. This is especially so in Formula Ford design, where the needs of many customers rather than the application of one specialised team will determine the car's performance.

In consequence, most of my seemingly good ideas are shot down before they stand much chance of fruition. The filter of practicality sifts out the non-starters at a very eary stage, and one is left with ostensibly workable schemes.

The initial concept will be achieved through various thought processes. First, it could simply be an inspirational notion based on that most valuable asset of the experienced designer — intuition. This intuitive feeling is a sixth sense that is developed through years of experience in designing and developing racing cars. It is the type of gift with which Colin Chapman was blessed. The inspiration was fired by the belief that existing known racing car technology could be pushed further by entering unknown areas of development.

With the basis of the design concept in mind, it would follow that some sort of preliminary investigation through model testing or rig testing would be advisable, before embarking on the manufacture of a totally new revolutionary solution. The correlation between model testing and simulated performance testing is getting closer all the time, as the engineer understands how to reproduce accurately the physical environment that is achieved full scale on varying circuits throughout the world.

In aircraft design, for example, one has only to place a scaled down aircraft in a model wind tunnel and apply varying mathematical rules concerning its scaled down effect. With a racing car, however, the race track is awash with very turbulent air and the car is changing its pitch, roll and yaw attitudes constantly. Therefore a stable aerodynamic balance is something which is very difficult to predict by modelling. One can only apply principles and hope that the advantage realises itself in the full scale application.

The Reynard 83 SF car was designed and conceived during the summer of 1981. In its initial form, as a Formula Ford 1600 car, the 83 SF made its first public appearance at the FF Festival at Brands Hatch in November. The car started with a clean sheet of paper, and was to be a combined 1600 and 2000 car. I believed that ground effect was unnecessary for Formula Ford 2000 in terms of cost and performance, and it made a lot of sense to produce one car which could do both formulas, rather than design two different cars and have to amortize tooling, jigging, and mould costs over lower production numbers. It also seemed logical that a former 1600 driver should be able to update his car to the two litre variety, should he desire. I believe this was one of the original reasons for introducing Formula Ford 2000.

The previous model that we had designed was in fact my first ever attempt at this category of racing car. It was based on my original 1974 FF design, and was subsequently updated until 1981, using the same basic chassis and component kit. Thus, updates were possible from one year to the next. I believe in not changing the car radically every year, but I thought that my car had

Side radiators mounted outside the chassis provide a simple solution to cooling problems. Note also the streamlined airbox and strong roll-over hoop on this FF2000 Reynard SF84. Like the rest of the distinctive rear end bodywork, the air box was developed aerodynamically.

Once a successful FF2000 driver himself, Reynard is sure that his own racing experience helps him considerably in interpreting crucial driver 'feedback'. Here he is in discussion with the promising young Brazilian, Maurizio Sandro Sala, who won the 1983 Esso Championship.

run out of development in 1981, and sales were lagging, and we needed a new model that would be capable of another five years of development.

My considerations for a new design were as follows:

1. It must out-perform all other racing cars currently being manufactured.

2. It must have about five years development potential.

3. It must be relatively low cost and easy to work on.

4. It must be very fast in a straight line, and have very low drag characteristics.

5. It must have a very stiff and strong chassis and any flexibility in components must be reduced to a minimum.

6. It must be able to be placed in production simply.

7. It must be very safe and strong in an accident, especially when rolled.

8. It must be built to a very high quality engineering standard.

I was able to achieve in the prototype most of these criteria, but I failed in certain areas.

First, the car as we ran it in its original guise overheated badly. In order to provide a quick and easy solution to this, we chose to mount the radiators externally to the stressed skin on the chassis. This meant cutting large holes into the outer skin of the chassis and we lost a lot of torsional stiffness immediately.

Secondly, we had a flexion problem at the back that showed up under braking, which caused tail wagging instability. We chased around during 1982 trying to eliminate this problem, but eventually I chose to redesign the complete back end, incorporating a twisting-blade rear anti-roll bar system, which was the basis of the 1983 car. We also chose not to use the dragless cooling system which had proven so difficult to persuade to function, and we mounted the radiators more forward and in the airstream exiting backwards.

The aerodynamics of the car have always been very good, and we chose to improve them during the 1983 season by testing on track and in the wind tunnel. A new FF2000 body system was developed in June 1983 as a result of those tests, which improved the downforce/drag ratio by about 15 per cent in the wind tunnel.

The suspension linkages and mechanisms

are a feature of the car which I have never chosen to alter. Perhaps surprisingly, I do not consider this function terribly important. I will try to eliminate any adverse steer effects or extreme changes during wheel movement, and I will try to make the track change as small as possible. However, I have no idea what type of Ackerman angle the car uses. I pay very little attention to camber change cures unless I cannot achieve a good car temperature balance at the circuit. I have never plotted a roll centre on any car that I have ever designed, front or rear, and I consider that any relative movement of roll centres is of very minor importance and is far outweighed by other dynamic changes that can be made to alter handling.

I pay very little attention to toe-in or toe-out settings, since all the tests that I have done have indicated that these make very little difference indeed. The castor angle I will alter simply to give a good steering feel, depending on the type of front tyre that is used on the car. The steering ratio is similarly developed, and I have never really played too much with anti-dive or anti-squat, but I will say that my existing car has approximately 15 per cent anti-dive at the front and zero anti-squat at the rear.

I consider the most important and overriding effect on vehicle handling is achieved by the balance of spring stiffness throughout the car. The vehicle is a complex mechanism of parallel and series inter-connected springs, and by achieving a correct balance of springs, front and rear, one can achieve the best handling performance and road holding grip. Of paramount importance in this equation is the stiffness of the chassis. Without a stiff chassis, no significant change will be noticed when varying spring stiffness front or rear.

1982 was a year when most of my concentration as a design engineer was focused towards the March Grand Prix team, of which I was chief engineer. The Reynard car in FF2000 form enjoyed some early successes, but never really realised its full potential. Following an end-of-season redesign, the prototype car was shipped to Florida and was tested in the gruelling heat for five solid days, where we were able to cover about 800 track miles. We had no yardstick concerning performance, but we were able to snag all the new systems on the car and also dial in some basic anti-roll bar, spring and damper setting that suited the American Goodyear tyres. Using the same basic settings, we later set a devastating time of 1m 5.4s on our first visit to

The distinctive Reynard tail treatment, unintentionally brought before the cameraman by driver excess. Note that even the underside of the car's mechanics is tucked away beneath smooth surfaces, intended to minimise turbulence and drag.

Stiff rear roll settings and softer front options encourage oversteer, as shown by Jeremy Rossiter in one of the earliest Reynard FF2000 challengers.

Snetterton, which was about a second under the lap record. With this encouraging start, we went on to achieve victory with the 83 SF model, with Tim Davies, in the 1983 British Championship. In fact, four of the top six places in the final points table belonged to Reynard drivers.

One of the most often asked questions during that year was why did I design a non-ground effect car, when over the previous two years ground-effect cars had won all races in Formula Ford 2000 and Formula Three? I suppose some of this philosophy was dictated by the fact that I wished the FF1600 car and FF2000 car to be the same basic layout. Probably more important was some of the wind tunnel experience that I enjoyed whilst doing Formula One with March. A ground-effect car, when working efficiently, simply has less drag and more downforce at a given speed than a car with conventional aerofoils. This however, is only effectively achieved when there is a good ground seal between the skirts and the surface of the road. If there is a consistent gap, as is required in

the regulations of Formula Three and Formula Ford 2000, then this efficiency drops off drastically, and the majority of suction effect is lost underneath the car. In addition to this, Vortex-type air flow is generated around the skirts of a car and on the underside, causing considerable drag. Any suction effect is also very variable, depending on the pitch attitude of the car. Consequently, handling characteristics are difficult to balance.

I have therefore used conventional aerofoils to develop a balanceable downforce, and have obtained a certain amount of extra downforce at little expense in terms of drag, by making the bodywork generate efficient downforce.

One of the most fascinating aspects of obtaining grip from a racing car at any circuit involves dialling in the tyre temperatures to maximise the grip of each tyre on the circuit. Each circuit has different cornering characteristics which impart different types of loadings on to the tyres. The tyre works best when it has a certain temperature spread across its surface from the outside to the inside. Any conventional tyre will

STATIC CAMBER SETTINGS

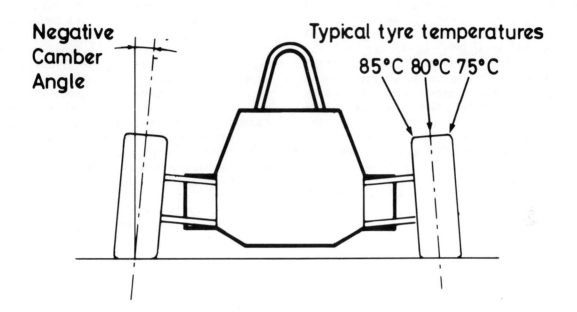

Negative Camber Angle

Typical tyre temperatures

85°C 80°C 75°C

CAR DURING ROLL (Too much camber on inside wheel)

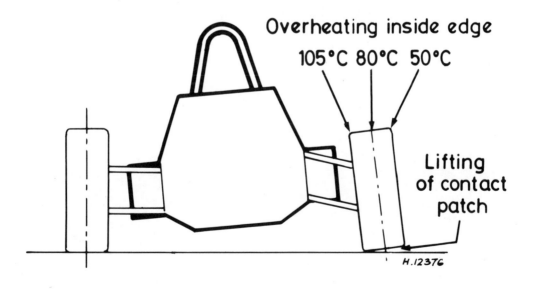

Overheating inside edge

105°C 80°C 50°C

Lifting of contact patch

H.12376

The effects of roll induced camber changes on tyre temperatures.

develop slightly more lateral cornering force when the top of the wheel/tyre is canted inwards towards the centreline of the car. This angle is called the camber angle. If all the wheels were perfectly vertical, then the camber angle would be zero. Tilting the wheels inward at the top is called negative camber, and tilting them outward is called positive camber (see Figure 1).

The reason that tyres produce slightly more grip when they run slightly negative camber is due to a constructional effect called camber thrust, which is effectively a sideways displacement of the contact patch of the elastic tyre. It is very easy however, to overcamber a tyre. This can entail the tyre running only on its inside edge, and the outside edge of the tyre will lose contact with the track, and thus the overall grip will be less (see Figure 2).

When a car rolls, the independent suspension of the type used on most current racing cars will partly compensate the roll of the chassis and keep the tyres more upright. However, if the geometry was designed to obtain total camber compensation for roll, then the wheels would be flapping up and down like butterfly wings whenever the car hits a bump.

I think it is unimportant whether a car has a high camber change rate and runs low static camber settings, or has very low camber changes but a lot of camber is wound on to achieve the correct tyre temperature spread. The middle of the tyre should ideally be an average between the two temperatures; if the middle of the tyre is too hot, then the inflation pressure is too hard.

The evolution of a successful racing car and its consequent developments will start on the first day it hits the track. I am a great believer in persevering with slightly unusual ideas even if the initial testing proves to be disappointing. However, most good designs will prove competitive immediately, with very little massaging to the springs, anti-roll bars, camber settings, etc. In development, I will try to obtain large chunks of performance by bolting on new components to try, rather than whittling away at tuneable items in order to obtain the perfect balance. Sometimes the quickest setting on the stop-watch doesn't relate to the most perfect balance that the driver wants. This enters another interesting area of performance development and possible gain in your Formula Ford racing — namely, the driver/engineer relationship. That, however, is another subject in itself...

9 The manufacturers

The manufacturers, quite literally, make Formula Ford. Sometimes, Formula Ford makes them. Just as often, it can break them.

Ever since the 500 cc Formula Three Coopers of the early 1950s, production line construction of racing cars has shown itself to be a business of potentially high rewards, but also high risks. In Formula Ford, as in all forms of motor racing, 'sales talk' counts for little in comparison with race results, and race results alone. Although clearly the most popular of all forms of participant motor racing, Formula Ford is also one of the most cut-and-thrust. Its market is fat, but fickle. On one weekend in Britain alone, there can be hundreds of FF cars racing — yet never have there been more than perhaps half-a-dozen manufacturers providing the competitive machinery.

Even amongst the most successful constructors, the health of race results and balance sheets is constantly changing. In the mid-1980s, marques such as Crosslé might seem to be drifting out of the limelight, while others, like Reynard, can almost be relied upon to steal an increasing part of the show. And it should always be remembered that there are permanent fringe efforts, cultivating talent and producing variety with marques such as Zeus, Quest, Jamun, Getem, Ray, Sparton, and Mondial. Fortunes can change dramatically from one season to the next, as the bumpy ups-and-downs of some of the most famous Formula Ford manufacturers show...

Reynard

It must seem a long, long time ago to Adrian Reynard that he had to steal to go racing. It is said there was a time when he had to make off with old railway lines under his coat, in order to rebuild his elderly and frequently crashed Ginetta G18B — a time that provides vivid contrast to his affluence today. But, in actual fact, it was only twelve years ago: twelve years in which 33 year old Reynard has achieved more than most designers *or* businessmen manage in a life time.

The story of Reynard Racing Cars is inevitably the story of its energetic source, Adrian Reynard. The history of Reynard Formula Ford cars did not really begin until 1973, and the story of their success has only been running since 1978, but this only serves to make the tale all the more impressive: in the five years since, Reynards have improved from home-brewed British also-rans to technically innovative world leaders. When one remembers the relative youth of Adrian Reynard, it is reasonable to expect that he will yet perform a few more dazzling designer's tricks to loud applause.

As a schoolboy, Reynard's mechanical and sporting interests were plain. He raced karts with success, went motorcycle scrambling, and later acted as mechanic to the late George Brown, a renowned speed record breaker on two wheels.

As a university student, reading Mechanical Engineering at Oxford, Adrian mixed his practical experience and academic abilities to design and build a record-setting bike of his own. Powered by a rare, two-stroke 250 cc Royal Enfield engine, which had been found especially for the project by Brown, this bike was ridden by Reynard to no less than five World Land Speed Records.

At much the same time, the energetic student also developed basic — and later essential — skills as an entrepreneur. By providing a welding service for colleagues' dilapidated automobiles, he was able to recoup the costs of running the bike. By maintaining this profitable sideline but

Adrian Reynard overstepping the mark.

also selling the sprint bike, he was able — at a pinch — to progress to Formula Ford.

To see just to what extent Reynard has progressed since in Formula Ford, one need look no further than the entrance foyer to a factory on the modern Telford Road Industrial Estate in Bicester: there, in the neighbourhood of two Grand Prix teams, Adrian has bought back his record bike and hung it on the wall of the factory. *His* factory, fully paid for.

Reynard, then, is not only a universally respected designer, but also an eminent Formula Ford industrialist. His pedigree even includes experience, and eventual success, as a single-seater racing driver. Whilst pursuing his British Leyland sponsored scholarship, Adrian found the time to drive that aged Ginetta in ten Formula Ford races. He recalls with amusement that he crashed nearly as often. *History* recalls that, though young Reynard's regular off-track excursions amplified his problem of inadequate finance, those reputedly stolen railway lines lead to ultimate respectability and wealth: in concluding that he could not afford to keep on re-building his car, and acutely aware that he couldn't afford a replacement either, Adrian decided to build his own car, from scratch. It was the start of Something Great.

Also in 1973, Reynard sowed the seeds of another business that would blossom: for a capital outlay of £60, he bought 50 per cent of a new fabricating venture, titled Sabre Automotive Ltd, with former March factory manager Bill Stone. Just eleven years later, the company approaches an annual turnover of £500,000, enjoys a profitability that is envied — and is now 90 per cent owned by Reynard. In addition to this, the Reynard Racing Cars Formulae Ford manufacturing business supports 22 full-time employees who generate a turnover of 'more than a million pounds'.

Yet it must be remembered that, even as recently as 1976, Reynard was virtually penniless. He illustrated that he was deserving of promotion, after a four year student apprenticeship and BL groundwork at Cowley, by placing his self-designed Formula Ford car in the parking bay of the Project Engineer at the Issigonis think-tank, at Longbridge. It made the right impression and he was soon appointed as chassis engineer, contributing to projects such as the Austin Princess and Mini Metro. But when Reynard became restless and sought promotion again, the answer this time was negative — so he left BL, and went to Cranfield to study for a Master's Degree in Vehicle Dynamics.

Before long, Reynard had also interrupted his concentrations on his studies, and went on the dole for a month in order to be able to afford a

Reynard returning unscathed from another early-career excursion with the remains of his car!

stand at the 1976 Racing Car Show. It was now his intention to become a fully committed racing car designer.

The boss of Hawke racing cars, Mike Keegan, brought that intention immediate fulfilment. He convinced Reynard that he should join his company, and Reynard duly convinced his tutor that the basis of his thesis should be Hawke's exciting long-term design project — a Formula One car!

The project, like the thesis, went unfinished. Keegan's racing driver son, Rupert, was invited to drive for Lord Hesketh's Grand Prix team in 1977, and that meant neither the Formula One car nor its designer were needed any more. Reynard was free — and more experienced, capable, and confident — to design Reynards.

Those designs achieved almost instant success. While the first few years of Reynard Racing Cars' history were devoted soley to FF2000 cars, the first few months were sufficient to indicate the talent of the company director. Along with his long-standing friend, Jeremy

Rossiter (once a tea boy for the Spax shock absorber company, now managing director), Adrian drove one of his new FF2000 cars in 1977. He not only managed to stay on the track more often, but also won three races and took five pole positions. He was plainly a young man who should be taken seriously.

Reynard's business demands were to be taken seriously as well, however, with the result that his racing efforts in 1978 were rather diluted. But in 1979, the tale was very different: to allow enough time at his director's desk, Adrian only raced in rounds of the European FF2000 Championship — and won it! Back home, Reynard-mounted David Leslie underlined the arrival of this gifted new designer by winning no less than fifteen out of thirty FF2000 races. At the same time Reynard began to accept that he is first and foremost a designer and company director: with the solitary exception of the 1981 New Zealand Formula Pacific series, he has not driven seriously since.

He has been worried seriously, however, for 99

like all manufacturers who concentrate on Formulae Ford's fat but fickle market he has teetered on the brink of bankruptcy. It was largely a consequence, he confesses, of being swept up by his startling success: in 1980, he went out and bought the new factory at Bicester, and boldly designed a no-compromise FF2000 ground-effects chassis. But the design was a radical failure. Without any exaggeration, Reynard recalls that he 'lost an absolute fortune'. Half the factory had to be let, and Adrian was forced to sell his house and car.

But the costly experience had its valuable lesson. 'Together', says Adrian, 'Formula Ford and the fabrication business form a wide based product, and that wide base has saved my company from bankruptcy on more than one occasion. That means I appreciate the importance of maintaining the wide base, until we're able to attract sufficient funds or sponsorship to secure our future in other forms of racing.

'The commercial success', he observes, 'isn't the complete goal in itself, but it's necessary to keep on producing ideas, to get there. That's been the underlying moral through all of my career.'

Get there Reynard has. 1980 can be forgotten as the difficult year of financial recovery, and remembered instead as the time in which Formula One introductions were made. Mid-season, Adrian was assigned to help the RAM team, struggling with Rupert Keegan in a privately run Williams FW07. Here, his design work impressed Team Manager John MacDonald sufficiently to be invited back again, to the RAM March fold, a year later. And here, says Adrian, 'the unending, constant desire to get in to Formula One at any expense was dispelled. It blew a few myths away.

'In terms of experience, F1 obviously taught me a lot. There was a wealth of new technology engineering expertise to work with, and it showed me what it was like to work with some of the finest professionals that I'd ever experienced throughout my career in motor racing, even though it wasn't the best team. I'm sure that, in coming back to work with my own company, it has raised the whole standard. And because the circumstances at March weren't extracting the best from me — because I could see how things were done badly as well as properly — I realised my future lies with a company in which I control

Reynard driving his first ever FF1600 design...

... and Scotsman David Leslie racing ahead in Reynard's first big time winner, in FF2000 in 1979.

the destiny. I've gone through a steep learning curve in the past few years, and thought it a good time to apply that knowledge to my own company.'

And so he has, with considerable effect. Although 1982 was not a year in which Reynards featured prominently in championship results, largely because the designer's attentions were directed elsewhere, 1983 witnessed a resurgence. Reynards took a 1-2-3 in the British FF2000 Championship, won the televised BBC 'Grandstand' series, scored a 1-2 in the FF1600 Festival, and enticed two leading FF1600 stars to abandon their Van Diemens mid-stream.

Overseas, expansion leaves Reynard's rivals trailing. Established markets are consolidated by Reynard and his dynamic Sales Manager, Rick Gorne, and new ones are established: in France, for instance, FF1600 was launched in 1984 as the first real challenger to Formule Renault — and the cars, constructed by Le Mans winners Rondeau, were based on the Reynard 83FF chassis.

In the Reynard factory, a £60,000 computer-operated machine tool facility had just been added to the company's armoury at the time of writing, and a carbonfibre Formula Three car — the first of its kind — was taking shape behind closed doors in readiness for an assault on the traditional Ralt

monopoly in 1985. Time does not stand still, and those days of destitution fade further away...

Royale

Royale Racing Ltd is one of Formula Ford's great survivors. The marque has enjoyed some glorious peaks during its history, and is second only to Van Diemen in the overall British Formula Ford championship victory tally. But is has also slumped in some troublesome troughs in its time, on occasion so deeply that its very existence seemed threatened. Even now, Royale is a racing car manufacturer with problems: at the time of writing, a season has just passed in which Royale conspicuously failed to feature in the top three positions in any of the numerous British national FF championships. In the three entire seasons before that, Royale didn't manage to win any British FF1600 titles at all.

Royale's directors have traditionally had a bumpy ride. The man now at the helm, 39 year old Alan Cornock, has seen his company fall uncontrollably into a descent, which started soon after designer Rory Byrne left the fold. The South African moved on in 1977 to work for Lola and then Toleman, leaving a void where before there had been a quite remarkable design talent.

Cornock, however, has overcome more

Former Royale van driver, turned director-owner, Alan Cornock.

serious difficulties in the past. Indeed, at the very moment that he assumed control of Royale Racing, in 1973, he must have feared its imminent collapse. The original Royale owner, Bob King, had simply been destroyed by the worries of the business. He retired after a nervous breakdown. Cornock inherited the untidy remnants of a small-sized constructor that had possibly been thinking too big. Royale had quickly diversified to become 'jacks' of many racing trades, but masters of none. Royale had expanded too, from modest premises in Park Royal (hence the name) to a brand new, 7,000 sq ft industrial unit at Huntingdon that it could barely afford. It had just boldly built a Formula Two car, intended for previous Royale driver and Super Vee Champion, Manfred Schurti, but could not afford to run that either. And on top of all this, it had the Oil Crisis, a national power crisis, and a crippling three day week to contend with.

In spite of these difficulties, contend Royale and Cornock did. And though there are serious problems arising from on-track mediocrity in the early 1980s, Royale will surely bounce back to Formula Ford prominence once again. The heat of the moment should not be allowed to obscure the achievement of years: look at the frequency of the name Royale in *The Champions* section, and a sense of perspective can be found.

The very first of the Royale founder's problems was without doubt also the funniest.

King had not only been a car salesman before he became a full-time racing engineer, but also an amateur racing driver. He competed in Cooper-Climax and, later, Lotus 24-Climax cars. He also prepared Climax engines. He was recognised as something of a specialist, and, to his great embarrassment, he was also recognised by his neighbours: legend tells that King not only tested client's cars on the public roads around his house, but also contrived to crash one through the window of the local off-licence! King's first problem was to leave the residents in peace and go and play somewhere else.

From the cramped garage behind his home, Bob King moved his business first to a base beneath Wembly Viaduct, in 1963 and then two years later, to Park Royal, NW10. Here, he formed Racing Preparations Ltd, a company title that would not be replaced by the Royale name until 1972, and source of the 'RP' prefix still attached to Royale model numbers today.

It was also at Park Royal that the present owner and director, Alan Cornock, joined the company. He remembers he was simply 'The Lad'. He also recalls with humour, 'I joined, for £7 per week, as the van driver, and then found out on my first day that I had to supply my own van!'

Another event of 1965 was Climax's clearance of its stocks. King bought the remaining pile of twin-cam engines, and his consequently prolific business, which included supplying race prepared engines to Formula One teams, gave Cornock the chance to show his organisational and administrative skills. Just eight years later, those skills enabled 'The Lad' to make Royale his own and save it from extinction.

Initially, Racing Preparations concentrated on engine tuning, although Climax engined cars such as Lotus 11s and Elites were not an uncommon source of work. King also chose to run an assortment of single-seaters, most notably for Tony Lanfranchi. By 1967, he had Formula Ford preparation work passing through his hands. But he was not impressed with what he saw. Whilst paying frequent attention to the race winning Alexis of Dave Morgan, he concluded that he could probably market a better Formula Ford car himself. And did.

That, logically, was the RP1. It was the first design provided for Royale, on a freelance basis, by Bob Marston — but it was by no means the last: twelve years later, the designer who went on to a senior post with Lola was *still* shaping Royales.

Marston's earlier Royale work, however, was plainly more successful. The RP1 prototype first took to the track on August 7, 1968, and eventually made its race debut at Brands Hatch, in the hands of current driver-trainer John Stevens, on January 19, 1969. (An earlier race attempt at the Brands Boxing Day meeting had to be abandoned with red faces when a shock absorber broke.) Within a few months, the RP2 production model had been built 40 times over — and sold out. No less than 37 models were shipped to the United States, but in Britain the Motor Racing Stables — entered example of Ray Allen scored notable success. In 1970, then, the updated RP3 inevitably also sold well.

Alas, in 1970 Royale also produced other things. King was occupied with a disastrously sudden bout of peripheral thinking. Models RP4 to RP15 were anything but Formula Fords, and almost anything but big money makers.

Of the more fruitful designs in this phase, the RP4 dominated the new F100 sports-racing category, with 1970 and '71 championships belonging to the Royales of Ray Allen and Tom Pryce, but the category itself was a poorly supported failure. The RP9 helped Liechtenstein's little Manfred Schurti on his way to the European Super Vee Championship, but also gave his sponsors over-ambitious ideas about turning to Formula Two. The RP11 Formula Three car profitably sold 15 copies after Pryce had given it a

sensational début victory at the 1971 Race of Champions meeting, and the RP12 Formula Atlantic derivative continued the popular Welshman's rise to fame. But of all the other brave ideas, ranging from a sports-racing F100 conversion to a stillborn Formula 5000 design and an aborted Formula Two project, Royale enjoyed little acclaim and less affluence. It was not until 1972 that the next Royale FF1600 car was built, and although it was a race winner it's emergence also coincided with the unwise move of premises to Huntingdon, the unsuccessful Formula Two idea, and the unhappy consequences of ten years' hard work and pressure on Bob King's health.

When Cornock bought the company in the realistic appreciation that no-one else would, there was a transformation in Royale's aims that divides the marque's life as clearly as a layer of sediment on sandstone. Only months after it had been proudly described as 'Britain's second largest racing car manufacturing business', Royale was moved quietly from its modern Huntingdon factory to an unglamorous, 4,000 sq ft building that had once been a Sergeant's Mess on the wartime Bomber Command station of Little

The successful seventies: 1977, and South African Rad Dougall is on his way to a double FF2000 championship victory for Royale.

The saviour of the Royale marque was the RP21, in 1975. Geoff Lees took the car to no less than three FF1600 championship wins, and Royale was back in business.

Staughton, Bedfordshire. Here, it was Cornock's immediate resolve to concentrate solely on the smaller engined single-seater formulas. It was the start, in other words, of the Royale Formula Ford renaissance.

Designer Rory Byrne was pivotal to that renaissance. He came to Europe with compatriot racing driver Roy Klomfass in pursuit of racing reward, and found it. By the end of 1974, his first design for Royale, the RP21, was ready to roll. A season had just dragged by in which, disastrously, a Royale hadn't won a single race, but in the season that followed, Geoff Lees took the RP21 to victories in all three of the British FF1600 championships, and won the Festival for the only time in Royale's entire history. Byrne's RP21 was Royale's saviour.

Since, the specialisation in FF1600 and 2000 has brought other titles, and provided rather more solid foundations to the Royale business. Most notably, Irishman Kenny Acheson swept to another three titles in 1978, Norfolkman David Sears took two slightly more junior series in 1979, and in FF2000 South African Rad Dougall won both British championships in 1977, with Briton Richard Trott repeating the feat three years later.

Byrne has gone on to dizzier heights, former Lola penman Pat Symonds has come and gone, and after a difficult period pioneering Formula Ford ground-effects, Bob Marston also joined Royale full-time and then left. Even Little Staughton and its crumbling airfield has been left behind, for in June 1980 Royale Racing moved to a 9,000 sq ft base on the site of a converted Bedfordshire village garage, in High Street, Riseley. There, the staff must reflect on another season of drought at the end of 1983, and must place their faith in yet another designer. At the time of writing it was Dutchman Wiet Huidekoper who has to provide the miracle cure... but at the time of editing this book, in February 1984, he, too, had left Royale...

Van Diemen

Van Diemen International Racing Services Ltd proved themselves capable of producing winning Formula Ford cars right from the start. That was in 1973, when former Jim Russell racing school mechanic turned self-employed race preparation

A lot to laugh about: once a mechanic with the Jim Russell Racing Drivers' School, Ralph Firman is now helmsman of one of the world's most successful production racing car manufacturers.

expert, Ralph Firman, made a vital decision. 'I couldn't see any future in my business', he recalls, 'other than doing the same thing, year in, year out. Then one morning I woke and thought 'Christ! I may as well build my own cars!' It seemed like the most natural thing in the world to do.'

Success came naturally, too, and quickly. The first Van Diemen, produced in rustic 1,000 sq ft premises at East Harling, Norfolk, was driven by Canadian Dave MacCallum in May 1973. But by June, Firman had enrolled the first in his long line of winning works drivers: Scotsman Don MacLeod put the Van Diemen FA73 on to pole position for its first heat as a factory entry, and then went on to win it. It is true that he also gyrated ignominiously out of the final that day, because of a faulty shock absorber, but this embarrassment was soon forgotten — by the season's end, MacLeod had won the BOC Championship. Van Diemen's winnings were instant credibility and crucial sales. Here was a manufacturer's success story with a quick start.

'After that first year', recalls Firman in his quiet Norfolk brogue, 'I decided, OK, I would go ahead and build 50 cars. I ordered construction materials, and shock absorbers, and welding

equipment, and this and that. When I sat back and looked at it all, I thought 'Oh God!', I couldn't believe it,' he laughs. 'I was suddenly a racing car manufacturer!'

It was not long before Firman's brave new venture was manufacturing him headaches. It would have been easy to see the early departure of the Norfolkman's original business partner, Ross Ambrose, as a wise decision. This Tasmanian racing driver had inspired the name of the marque (Tasmania was once known as Van Diemen's Land), but he didn't stay on long enough to inspire much else: when the business encountered its first worrying problems, they belonged to Firman and his present co-director, and wife, Angie.

Problems there were, for although the début 1973 season had been tremendously encouraging, it had flattered largely to deceive. The following year saw Formula Three refugee Bernard Vermilio score individual race successes for Van Diemen, but the real star of the show was usually Richard Morgan — in a Crosslé. There were three different FF1600 championships in Britain that year, and they became the proud property of three different manufacturers. Van Diemen was not among them.

1975 wasn't any better. With the passing of each race, the dream début of Firman's first car became more distant, the hard commercial rules of Formula Ford more clear: if you do not win, you do not sell, and you do not attract the best of the drivers who are capable of winning...

Van Diemen's was a problem verging on crisis.

Dave Baldwin's was a design talent which provided the solution. Local to the Norfolk born and bred car constructor, he came to Van Diemen with experience that included recent Formula One stints at Ensign and Emerson Fittipaldi's Copersucar team. In 1976, he agreed to work for Firman on a consultancy basis. He also worked wonders: before the season was over, Van Diemen had been able to provide the re-hired Don MacLeod with a car in which he managed to win his heat, quarter-final, and semi-final of the Formula Ford Festival. The works run Van Diemen even challenged Derek Daly's Hawke for the lead of the final as well, until MacLeod spun away any possible hopes of victory.

Early in 1976, Daly had been one of several leading drivers who had abandoned a Van Diemen chassis in surprised dissatisfaction. By 1977, with the memories of that end-of-season Festival still fresh, drivers were swapping back again.

Van Diemen's markedly changed fortunes were represented convincingly in 1977 by factory driver Chico Serra. The Brazilian enjoyed the sort of season that suggested he was on his way to Grands Prix fame; Firman enjoyed the sort of

Van Diemen's RF77 and the skills of Chico Serra represented a highlight in the marque's history, interrupting rather too many low points.

commercial recovery that leaves 1977 as a particularly memorable year in the history of Van Diemen. Serra, he insists, was one of the most talented drivers he has ever run, and 'largely underrated'. And the RF77 model, he admits, was a highlight in his company's record. 'I think that *every* year has a highlight if we bring out a new car', explains Firman, 'but 1977 was certainly a particular highlight. We'd come to the end of the road with the car I'd cobbled up and put together in 1973, and when Dave agreed to design a replacement it was definitely a turning point.'

Since turning, there has been no need to look back. Excepting a spell when former BRM penman Mike Pilbeam freelanced for Van Diemen, Baldwin has remained a significant ingredient in the East Anglian marque's success. He has been a shareholder of the company since 1978, and a full-time employee since 1980, which Firman says 'was as soon as we could afford him.' He has also conceived Formula Ford cars whose track record no other single manufacturer has been able to match. In the decade since 1974, Van Diemens have taken more meaningful FF1600 titles than any other make. These have included no less than four successes in the prestigious Formula Ford Festival, and the same number of victories in not only the Townsend Thoresen and P&O, but also the Dunlop/*Autosport* championships, as well as three claims to the RAC series. Of that impressive total of 19 titles, only Royale can stand up to any serious comparison, with 11.

Since the start of the eighties, Firman and Baldwin have made more serious efforts also to include the Van Diemen name in the championship tables of FF2000. Yet again they have enjoyed prompt reward: ebullient Irishman Tommy Byrne, a sometime Grand Prix driver for the Theodore team, won the British and European FF2000 titles in a works Van Diemen in 1981. The following year, highly acclaimed Brazilian Ayrton Senna, who is now a Grand Prix regular with Toleman, repeated this achievement for the factory, chased hard in both series by the privately run Van Diemen of Calvin Fish. And although 1983 was a year in which the paddock talk was of Reynards, Baldwin was simultaneously penning 1984 models that illustrated Van Diemen's resolve to

The inspiration behind the Van Diemen designs, Dave Baldwin.

fight back. 'Of the 774 cars we've produced and sold so far', explains Firman, 'only a very, very small proportion have been two-litre cars. The bias towards 1600s is still very high — about 70 per cent — but that's not saying we can't see a changing market. 2000 is getting bigger and better all the time, and obviously we think it's important to be a big part of it.'

That intention should almost be taken for granted. Results alone show how seriously Van Diemens must nearly always be reckoned with. Indeed, Firman will even confess that perhaps nowadays his marketing relies too much on that fine track record. It is possibly *off* the circuit, he says, where he is losing ground in the early 1980s — where it is most notably Adrian Reynard and Rick Gorne who are winning the respect and remuneration of overseas markets.

So yes, the competition that faces Van Diemen gets tougher all the time. The sort of competition that Firman thrives on. He is less likely to perceive the pressure than he is the signs of his success. It *is* nice owning a brand new Mercedes when all you once used to possess was a tool box, and it can only be pleasing to drive that Mercedes to your *own* factory in the mornings. From East Harling in 1973, to two war-built Nissen huts just across the road from Snetterton Circuit in 1974, Van Diemen's operations are now based on that same Snetterton site in a modern,

30,000 sq ft industrial unit. Mr and Mrs Firman co-direct 14 employees full-time, and 'field out enough fabrication work to keep another 50 people in work all year round.' The run a business with an annual turnover quoted as £850,000, and with a profitability that is unquestionable. Obvious benefactors of Van Diemen cars have been a list of drivers that includes Chico Serra, Raul Boesel, Jonathan Palmer, Ayrton Senna, Tommy Byrne, Mike Thackwell, and Roberto Moreno. But the greatest benefactor of all has been Formula Ford itself, in which Van Diemen has been, and will doubtless continue to be, an integral and influential part.

Lola

It is true that Lola Cars Ltd is not so readily thought of as a Formula Ford manufacturer as are Van Diemen, or Royale, or Reynard. It might even seem that, throughout much of the 25 years since its inception, Lola has achieved renown with almost every sort of racing car but Formula Fords. From an 1172 cc Ford Special in 1957, Lola has gone on to produce and sell over 2,000 cars and no less than 80 different model types. These have ranged from Formula Junior to Formula One, from two-litre Sports racers to Can-Am and Group C winners, and from America-bound Super Vees to victors at Indianapolis. The designs have taken the Lola company from a lock-up garage, behind the founder's family tailoring business in Bromley, to a highly equipped, 23,000 sq ft factory, on an industrial estate in Glebe Road, Huntingdon.

It is only since 1976 that the Lola badge has appeared on Formula Fords — but it is also only to be expected that these cars were winners. In 1981 and 1982 in particular, Lolas were capable of mixing with, and often defeating, the best of the very good bunch that always comprises Formula Ford 1600.

Lola's founder and chief designer, Eric Broadley, has regularly produced innovative and successful racing cars. Those who have worked closely with this softly-spoken hard-thinker will argue energetically that he is a man whose genius often goes unnoticed, or at the very least under rated. Right from the start, they will remind you, Broadley was capable of beating the likes of Colin Chapman: three years after he raced a 750 Special shared with his cousin, Graham, Broadley designed and built his own 1172 cc Ford Special, with some machining help from a friend called Bob Rushbrook. Straight away, the car was a winner. Even in the hands of Broadley, the first Lola could destroy the long-standing monopoly held by Chapman's Lotus XIs.

Broadley would be quick to admit that he was probably not the most gifted racing driver the world has ever seen. His frustrated track rivals

108   *A designer who can be credited with many winning racing cars beyond the bounds of Formula Ford, Eric Broadley.*

The Lola factory.

were equally quick to reach this conclusion: by the end of the 1958 season, they were queueing up in request of Lola replicas. It was all the encouragement the trained architect needed to abandon his job with a large construction firm and become a professional racing car constructor. Rushbrook continued to assist with Lola production, and today he is a director of the company, and works manager. And the company itself has not only won on the track, but in commerce. It is no mean feat to be Britain's longest-established racing car producer, still operating profitably after a quarter-of-a-century. Unlike almost any other manufacturer of Formula Fords one cares to mention, Lola has never really had to scrabble desperately on the edge of the financial abyss.

The recent, increasingly apparent interest of Lola in the Ford formulas emphasises the company's head-over-heart business approach. As competitions director and former Williams Grand Prix Team Manager, Jeff Hazell, admitted in the pages of *Motoring News* in 1983, 'We feel it is important to make FF1600 cars because it keeps our workforce fully occupied, and it gives our junior designers the opportunity to assume responsibility for cars. They can attend a lot of races close to home to give help to customers and our works-assisted cars, while at the same time expanding their experience.'

Lola also likes to point out that its wide-spread design and production philosophy has a further benefit for Formula Ford customers. 'If, on our initiative, we created an F1 team,' explains Hazell, 'we would have to extend our own resources so much we would endanger our long-term future, and we're not prepared to take that risk. One of the main attractions of buying a car from us is that the customer knows we'll still be in business next year, and so he will still be able to buy spares, or have an up-date. He does not have that degree of security with every company selling racing cars.'

Perhaps that vaunted degree of security pales into insignificance when compared to Formula Ford's strongest selling point, which is not after-sales service tomorrow, but competitiveness today. But on this premise, too, Lola has its attractions: in 1981, the marque won the BARC Junior Championship with Mark Peters, a success it repeated in the BP Superfind Junior

Although it is easy to think of Lola as constructors of almost anything but Formula Fords, its track record in the junior single-seater category is impressive. Andrew Gilbert-Scott won both the RAC and Townsend Thoresen series for the Huntingdon based marque in 1983.

Championship two years later with Graham de Zille. In 1982, up-and-coming Briton, Julian Bailey, won the FF Festival and the tough Townsend Thoreson Championship, and in 1983 Andrew Gilbert-Scott's Lola won the TT series again, as well as the RAC title.

It is still unclear to this day where the name Lola itself actually came from. Unreliable legend has it that Eric Broadley's wife dreamt up the tag during one of the many long nights when her husband was working away in the garage, prompted by the popular hit song with its line 'Whatever Lola wants, Lola gets'! But it is perfectly clear, for all to see, that Lola's participation in the junior Ford formulas is increasing. More so than ever before, whatever success Lola FF drivers want, they are likely to get...

Crosslé

In Britain at least, John Crosslé's name seems to be gradually slipping from view, his most glorious days a fading memory. But that is certainly not to say that Crosslé racing cars should yet be dismissed: lest we should forget, Crosslé has on occasion played a very dominant role in British Formula Ford racing, not least in 1976, when David Kennedy won both the Townsend Thoresen and RAC Championships for the marque.

Like Lola founder Eric Broadley, Crosslé's initial design talent was weaned on the inexpensive 1172 cc Ford Specials of the late 1950s. Unlike Broadley, however, John did not forsake his own driving activities as soon as there was a demand for replicas of his car. Previously a motorcycle racer, and the winner of the Irish national Grass Track Championships for three years in succession, Crosslé continued racing whilst also constructing cars, and won the coveted Ford of Ireland Competition in one of his own 1172 cc Specials, in 1962. And at much the same time, the Crosslé workshop opened, in modest premises behind John's grey, brick-built house in Knocknagoney, County Down, an area where his family previously farmed.

Since, Crosslé has been famous for producing a diversity of racing machinery, including cars for Formula Junior, Sports Racing, Formula Three,

Like Irishman David Kennedy and Kenny Acheson, South African Desiré Wilson spent some of her early career in Formula Fords built by Crosslé.

some beefy Formule Libre contenders, and even Formula 5000. In the late 1960s, Crosslé's drivers included a promising young Irishman by the name of John Watson, and just over a decade later they added the successful Formula Ford names of Kennedy and Kenny Acheson to the list. Although the latter's tremendous string of FF1600 victories came only after he had switched to a works Royale, the effervescent Kennedy's 1976 championship double was probably the highlight of Crosslé's history. Prior to that, the Irish constructor had provided the car in which the late Gerry Birrell won the 1969 European FF Championship, while Richard Morgan led home a Crosslé 1–2 at the 1974 FF Festival, and won the Wella Championship as well.

In the eight years that have followed Kennedy's success, Crosslés have become a rare part of Formula Ford results sheets, but the sixth place of a recent Crosslé 55F in the 1983 Festival showed that the name is by no means extinct.

Appendix 1
The champions

Formula Ford Festival winners

1972
1. Ian Taylor (Dulon LD9)
2. Derek Lawrence (Titan Mk 6)
3. Larry Perkins (Elfin England)
4. David Loring (Merlyn Mk 20A)
5. Danny Sullivan (Elden Mk8)
6. Patrick Neve (Merlyn Mk 20A)

1973
1. Derek Lawrence (Dulon MP15)
2. Donald MacLeod (Van Diemen FA73)
3. Syd Fox (Hawke DL11)
4. Robert Arnott (Merlyn Mk24)
5. Graham Cuthbert (Van Diemen FA73)
6. Richard Hawkins (Titan Mk6)

1974
1. Richard Morgan (Crosslé 25F)
2. Frank Hopper (Crosslé 25F)
3. Roy Klomfass (Hawke DL12)
4. Richard Hawkins (Dulon MP 15B)
5. Bernard Vermilio (Van Diemen RF74)
6. Jim Walsh (Van Diemen RF74)

1975
1. Geoff Lees (Royale RP21)
2. Mike Blanchet (Crosslé 30F)
3. Rad Dougall (Royale RP21)
4. Rod Bremner (Crosslé 30F)*
5. Peter White (Royale RP21)
6. John Bright (Royale RP21)
*First on the road, but penalised 10 seconds for jumping start.

1976
1. Derek Daly (Hawke DL17)
2. Derek Warwick (Hawke DL17)
3. Rick Morris (Hawke DL15)
4. Rod Bremner (Crosslé 30F)
5. Kenny Gray (Royale RP21)
6. David Kennedy (Crosslé 30F)

1977
1. Chico Serra (Van Diemen RF77)
2. David Leslie (Royale RP24)
3. Trevor van Rooyen (Royale RP24)
4. Mike Blanchet (Lola T540)
5. Donald MacLeod (Van Diemen RF77)
6. Kenny Acheson (Crosslé 32F)

1978
1. Michael Roe (Van Diemen RF78)
2. James Weaver (Van Diemen RF78)
3. Terry Gray (Royale RP24)
4. Donald MacLeod (Sark 1)
5. Peter Morgan (Lola T540)
6. Joe Greenan (Crosslé 30F)

1979
1. Donald MacLeod (Sark 2)
2. Terry Gray (Van Diemen RF79)
3. Rick Morris (PRS RH01)
4. David Sears (Royale RP26)
5. Richard Morgan (Crosslé 32F)
6. Robert Gibbs (Royale RP26)

1980

1. Roberto Moreno (Van Diemen RF80)
2. Tommy Byrne (Van Diemen RF80)
3. Rick Morris (Royale RP28)
4. Jonathan Palmer (Van Diemen RF80)
5. David Coyne (Royale RP26)
6. Robert Gibbs (Van Diemen RF80)

1981

1. Tommy Byrne (Van Diemen RF81)
2. Rick Morris (Royale RP29)
3. James Weaver (Reynard FF82)
4. Robert Gibbs (Van Diemen RF81)
5. John Village (Royale RP29)
6. David Wheeler (Royale RP29)

1982

1. Julian Bailey (Lola T640)
2. Rick Morris (Royale RP31M)
3. John Pratt (Lola (T640)
4. Keith Fine (Royale RP31)
5. Uwe Schafer (Ray 82F)
6. Anthony Reid (Van Diemen RF82)

1983

1. Andrew Gilbert-Scott (Reynard 83FF)
2. Andrew Wallace (Reynard 83FF)
3. John Pratt (Lola T642E)
4. Mark Newby (Van Diemen RF83)
5. Antonio Albacete (Van Diemen RF83)
6. Anthony Murray (Crosslé 55F)

Derek Daly, a race winner in 1976, but overshadowed by his compatriot David Kennedy. Both were tremendously successful in Formula Ford, both eventually reached Grands Prix, but since neither have enjoyed much success!

South African Trevor van Rooyen, a Royale seated RAC Championship winner in 1977.

Kenny Acheson, waving the flag for Royale in the RP26. Later (1983) a RAM Grand Prix driver.

One of Formula Ford's popular — and fast — veterans, Rick Morris, in a 1982 Royale, winning the Silverstone based Esso Championship.

Formula Ford 1600 Champions

1968
Guards Championship
1. Tim Schenken (Merlyn)
2. Tony Trimmer (Brabham)
3. Claude Bourgoignie (Lotus)

1969
Les Leston Championship
1. Dave Walker (Lotus)
2. Tony Trimmer (Titan)
3. Mo Harness (Lotus)

1970
Les Leston Championship
1. Colin Vandervell (Merlyn)
2. Geddes Yeates (Merlyn)
3. Bernard Vermilio (Merlyn)

1971
BOC Championship
1. Bernard Vermilio (Merlyn)
2. Tony Brise (Merlyn/Elden)
3. Russell Wood (Merlyn)

1972
BOC Championship
1. Ian Taylor (Dulon)
2. Derek Lawrence (Titan)
3. Bob Arnott (Merlyn)

Sunbeam Electric Championship
1. Syd Fox (Hawke)
2. Ken Bailey (Titan)
3. Derek Lawrence (Titan)

Daily Express Championship
1. Ian Taylor (Dulon)
2. Derek Lawrence (Titan)
3. Keith Garratt (Lotus)

1973
BOC Championship
1. Don MacLeod (Van Diemen)
2. Bob Arnott (Merlyn)
3. Frank Hopper (Crosslé)

STP Championship
1. Derek Lawrence (Titan)
2. Don MacLeod (Van Diemen)
3. Richard Hawkins (Titan)

Wella for Men Championship
1. Ted Wentz (Elden)
2. Roger Manning (Elden)
3. Stephen South (Ray)

1974
British Oxygen Golden Helmet Championship
1. Syd Fox (Hawke)
2. Stephen South (Ray)
3. Mike Young (Merlyn/Van Diemen)

STP Championship
1. Patrick Neve (Lola)
2. Geoff Lees (Royale)
3. Bernard Vermilio (Merlyn)

Wella for Men Championship
1. Richard Morgan (Ray/Crosslé)
2. Tiff Needell (Elden))
3. Syd Fox (Hawke)

1975
British Air Ferries Championship
1. Geoff Lees (Royale)
2. Rick Morris (Hawke)
3. Jim Walsh (Hawke)

Brush Fusegear Championship
1. Geoff Lees (Royale)
2. Matthew Argenti (Van Diemen)
3. Jim Walsh (Royale)

National Organs Championship
1. Geoff Lees (Royale)
2. Kenny Gray (Van Diemen)
3. Rad Dougall (Royale)

1976
Brush Fusegear Championship
1. Jim Walsh (Royale)
2. Matthew Argenti (Van Diemen/Royale)
3. Derek Warwick (Hawke)

DJM Records Championship
1. Rod Bremner (Crosslé)
2. Derek Warwick (Hawke)
3. Jim Walsh (Royale)

RAC Championship
1. David Kennedy (Crosslé)
2. Derek Warwick (Hawke)
3. Kenny Gray (Royale)

Townsend Thoresen Championship
1. David Kennedy (Crosslé)
2. Kenny Gray (Royale)
3. Rick Morris (Hawke)

Dunlop Star of Tommorow Championship
1. Sean Walker (Royale)
2. David Leslie (Crosslé)
3. Nigel Mansell (Hawke)

Geoff Lees/Royale, second in the STP Championship, 1974. Later European Formula Two Champion for Ralt-Honda.

Richard Morgan, 1974 Wella for Men Champion, pictured in 1973.

Derek Warwick was second in two championships in 1976 despite running on the proverbial shoestring. No money worries nowadays, as team mate to Patrick Tambay at Renault.

1977

BARC Championship
1. David Leslie (Royale)
2. David McClelland (Crosslé)
3. Nigel Mansell (Crosslé/Javelin)

Brush Fusegear Championship
1. Nigel Mansell (Crosslé/Javelin)
2. Trevor van Rooyen (Royale)
3. Michael Roe (Van Diemen)

RAC Championship
1. Trevor van Rooyen (Royale)
2. Chico Serra (Van Diemen)
3. Yves Sarazin (Royale)

Townsend Thoresen Championship
1. Chico Serra (Van Diemen)
2. Donald MacLeod (Van Diemen)
3. David Leslie (Royale)

Dunlop Star of Tommorrow Championship
1. Willy T. Ribbs (Royale)
2. Bill Shepherd (Crosslé)
3. Terry Blanchet (Royale)

1978

Esso Championship
1. Peter Morgan (Lola)
2. Jim Walsh (Royale)
3. Bernard Devaney (PRS)

Philips Car Radio Championship
1. Kenny Acheson (Royale)
2. David McClelland (Van Diemen)
3. David Sears (Royale)

RAC Championship
1. Kenny Acheson (Royale)
2. Michael Roe (Van Diemen)
3. Bernard Devaney (PRS)

Townsend Thoresen Championship
1. Kenny Acheson (Royale)
2. Michael Roe (Van Diemen)
3. David McClelland (Van Diemen)

Dunlop Star of Tomorrow Championship
1. Rob Zurrer (Crosslé/PRS)
2. Terry Gray (Royale)
3. Mike Thackwell (Van Diemen)

Also a champion in '77, current Lotus Grand Prix driver, Nigel Mansell.

Michael Roe (Van Diemen), second in the Townsend Thoresen and RAC series in 1978, now a professional racing driver in the United States. Being chased by David Leslie.

1979
Esso Championship
1. Jim Walsh (Royale)
2. Cameron Binnie (Van Diemen)
3. Richard Trott (Royale)

P&O Ferries Championship
1. David Sears (Royale)
2. Terry Gray (Van Diemen)
3. Jonathan Palmer (Van Diemen)

RAC Championship
1. David Sears (Royale)
2. Fernando Ribeiro (Van Diemen)
3. Jim Walsh (Royale)

Townsend Thoresen Championship
1. Terry Gray (Van Diemen)
2. James Weaver (Tiga)
3. Jonathan Palmer (Van Diemen)

Dunlop Star of Tomorrow Championship
1. Guy Dormehl (Van Diemen)
2. Martin Holman (Royale)
3. Keith Wiggins (Royale)

1980
Esso Championship
1. Jim Walsh (Royale)
2. David Wheeler (Royale)
3. Tom Wood (Van Diemen)

P&O Ferries Championship
1. Tommy Byrne (Van Diemen)
2. David McClelland (Van Diemen)
3. Luiz Schaffer (Van Diemen)

RAC Championship
1. Tommy Byrne (Van Diemen)
2. Raul Boesel (Van Diemen)
3. Rick Morris (Royale)

Townsend Thoresen Championship
1. Roberto Moreno (Van Diemen)
2. Raul Boesel (Van Diemen)
3. Jonathan Palmer (Royale/Van Diemen)

Dunlop Star of Tomorrow Championship
1. Tim Lee-Davey (Tiga)
2. David Coyne (Royale)
3. Andrew Gilbert-Scott (Van Diemen)

BRSCC Pre '74 Championship
1. Andy Wallace (Hawke)
2. Simon Davey (Dulon)
3. Peter Bell (Elden)

1981
Esso Championship
1. John Village (Royale)
2. David Wheeler (Royale)
3. Andy Wallace (Royale)

P&O Ferries Championship
1. Enrique Mansilla (Van Diemen)
2. Robert Gibbs (Van Diemen)
3. David Wheeler (Royale)

RAC Championship
1. Ayrton Senna da Silva (Van Diemen)
2. Rick Morris (Royale)
3. Enrique Mansilla (Van Diemen)

Townsend Thoresen Championship
1. Ayrton Senna da Silva (Van Diemen)
2. Rick Morris (Royale)
3. Alfonso Toledano (Van Diemen)

Dunlop/Autosport Star of Tomorrow Championship
1. Phil Kempe (Royale)
2. Mark Peters (Lola)
3. Karl Jones (Royale)

BARC Junior Championship
1. Mark Peters (Lola)
2. Robert Meaton (Royale)
3. Kenny Andrews (Van Diemen)

BRSCC Pre '74 Championship
1. Simon Davey (Dulon)
2. Tony Sinclair (Ray)
3. Craig Dennis (Lotus)

1982
Esso Championship
1. Rick Morris (Royale)
2. { Andy Wallace (Van Diemen)
     John Village (Royale)

P&O Ferries Championship
1. Gianfranco Cané (Van Diemen)
2. Dave Hunt (Van Diemen)
3. David Wheeler (Royale)

RAC Championship
1. Mauricio Gugelmin (Van Diemen)
2. Julian Bailey (Lola)
3. Rick Morris (Royale)

Townsend Thoresen Championship
1. Julian Bailey (Lola)
2. Mauricio Gugelmin (Van Diemen)
3. Rick Morris (Royale)

*Dunlop/Autosport Star of Tomorrow
Championship*
1. John Penfold (Van Diemen)
2. Paul Mather (Royale)
3. Andy Middlehurst (Van Diemen)

BP Superfind Junior Championship
1. Mark Newby (Royale/Van Diemen)
2. Paul Mather (Royale)
3. Andy Middlehurst (Van Diemen)

BRSCC Pre '74 Championship
1. Steve Bradley (Van Diemen)
2. Pete Rogers (Merlyn)
3. Gareth Lloyd (Dulon)

1983
Esso Championship
1. Maurizio Sandro Sala (Van Diemen/Reynard)
2. Andy Wallace (Van Diemen/Reynard)
3. Antonio Albacete (Van Diemen)

P&O Ferries Championship
1. Peter Hardman (Van Diemen)
2. Andy Middlehurst (Van Diemen)
3. Andrew Gilbert-Scott (Lola)

RAC Championship
1. Andrew Gilbert-Scott (Lola)
2. { Andy Wallace (Van Diemen/Reynard)
{ Maurizio Sandro Sala (Van Diemen/Reynard)

Townsend Thoresen Championship
1. Andrew Gilbert-Scott (Lola)
2. Mark Peters (Van Diemen)
3. John Pratt (Lola)

*Dunlop/Autosport Star of Tomorrow
Championship*
1. Perry McCarthy (Van Diemen)
2. John Robinson (Ray)
3. Bernard Horwood (Lola)

BP Superfind Junior Championship
1. Graham de Zille (Lola)
2. Peter Rogers (Van Diemen)
3. Peter Rose (Lola)

BRSCC Pre '74 Championship
1. Paul Sleeman (Rostron)
2. Chris Woodcock (Dulon)
3. David Porter (Elden)

1983 Esso Champion and 1984 FF2000 graduate, Maurizio Sandro Sala.

Man of the moment, Andrew Gilbert-Scott.

Formula Ford 2000 Champions

1975
Allied Polymer Championship
1. Derek Lawrence (Crosslé)
2. Bernard Vermilio (Merlyn)
3. Ian Taylor (Dulon)

1976
Allied Polymer Championship
1. Ian Taylor (Dulon)
2. Tiff Needell (Hawke)
3. Geoff Friswell (Hawke)

1977
Lord's Taverners Championship
1. Rad Dougall (Royale)
2. Jeremy Rossiter (Reynard)
3. Kenny Gray (Royale)

British Air Ferries Championship
1. Rad Dougall (Royale)
2. Jeremy Rossiter (Reynard)
3. Philip Bulman (Hawke)

1978
Lord's Taverners Championship
1. Syd Fox (Palliser)
2. David Leslie (Van Diemen)
3. Mike Blanchet (Lola)

British Air Ferries Championship
1. Mike White (Delta)
2. David Leslie (Van Diemen)
3. Syd Fox (Palliser)

1979
ShellSport/Martini Championship
1. David Leslie (Reynard)
2. Simon Kirkby (Reynard)
3. Tim Wallwork (Reynard)

Computacar Championship
1. David Leslie (Reynard)
2. Peter Morgan (Lola)
3. Simon Kirkby (Reynard)

1980

Motorcraft Championship
1. Richard Trott (Royale)
2. Tim Davies (Reynard/Royale)
3. Rob Cooper (Lola)

Imperial Leather Classic Championship
1. Richard Trott (Royale)
2. Mike Taylor (Royale)
3. Rob Cooper (Lola)

1981

Pace British Championship
1. Tommy Byrne (Van Diemen)

2. Simon Kirkby (Royale/Reynard)
3. Mike Taylor (Royale)

1982

Pace British Championship
1. Ayrton Senna da Silva (Van Diemen)
2. Calvin Fish (Royale/Van Diemen)
3. Kenny Andrews (Van Diemen)

1983

Racing Displays British Championship
1. Tim Davies (Reynard)
2. Mauricio Gugelmin (Van Diemen)
3. Julian Bailey (Reynard)

Appendix 2
Business directory

Circuits

Aintree: Aintree Circuit Club Ltd, 204 Muirhead Avenue, Liverpool 13. Tel: 051-256 0366.
Contact: Club Secretary, Colin Brady.

Brands Hatch: Brands Hatch Circuit Ltd, Fawkham, Dartford, Kent DA3 8NG. Tel: (0474) 872331. Telex: 96172.
Contact: Promotions Director, Robin Bradford.

Cadwell Park: Cadwell Park International Racing Circuit, Old Manor House, Cadwell Park, Louth, Lincs LN11 9SE. Tel: (050 784) 248.
Contact: Circuit Manager, Chas Wilkinson.

Castle Combe: Castle Combe Circuit Ltd, 140 Bristol Road, Frampton Cotterell, Bristol BS17 2AX. Tel: (0454) 773014.
Contact: Managing Director, Howard Strawford.

Croft: Croft Autodrome Ltd, Dalton, Darlington, Co. Durham DL2 2PL. Tel: (0325) 720206.
Contact: Circuit Manager, L. R. Dixon-Cade.

Donington Park: Donington Park Racing Ltd, Castle Donington, Derby DE7 5RP. Tel: (0332) 810048. Telex: 377793.
Contact: Managing Director, Robert Fearnell.

Kirkistown: 500 Motor Racing Club of Ireland Ltd, 2b Mount Merrion Avenue, Belfast BT6 0FR. Tel: (0232) 692863.
Contact: Club Secretary.

Lydden: Lydden Motor Racing Circuit, William Mark Holdings Ltd, 71 West Street, Sitting-bourne, Kent ME10 1AN. Tel: (0304) 830557 on race days or (0795) 72926.
Contact: Circuit Manager, Frank Phipps.

Mallory Park: Mallory Park Circuit Ltd, Kirkby Mallory, Leicester LE9 7QE. Tel: (0455) 42931/2.
Contact: Edwina Overend.

Mondello Park: Motor Racing Circuits Ltd, 58 Haddington Road, Dublin 4. Tel: Dublin 681355. Telex: 31561.
Contact: Managing Director, Stuart Cosgrave.

Oulton Park: Cheshire Car Circuit Ltd, Oulton Park, Little Budworth, Tarporley, Cheshire CW6 9BW. Tel: (082921) 301/2.
Contact: Circuit Manager, Dorothy Knox.

Pheonix Park: Irish Motor Racing Club Ltd, 12 Robins Villas, Palmerstown, Dublin 20. Tel: Dublin 983830.
Contact: Club Secretary.

Scotcircuit (formerly Ingliston): Scotcircuit Ltd, PO Box 5, 25 Market Square, Duns, Berwickshire TD11 3EQ. Tel: (03612) 3724.
Contact: Chairman, Graham Hamilton.

Silverstone: Silverstone Circuits Ltd, Silverstone, Towcester, Northants NN12 8TN. Tel: (0327) 857271. Telex: 311164.
Contact: Marketing and Communications Manager, Juliette Slaughter.

Snetterton: Snetterton Circuit Ltd, Snetterton, Norwich, Norfolk NR16 2JU. Tel: (095387) 303.
Contact: Circuit Director, Bob Ross.

Thruxton: Thruxton (BARC) Ltd, Thruxton Circuit, Andover, Hants. Tel: (026 477) 2696/7. Telex: 47591 BARCTX G.
Contact: Circuit Manager, Warwick Offord.

Clubs

British Automobile Racing Club, Thruxton Motor Racing Circuit, Thruxton, Andover, Hants. Tel: (026 477) 2607 or 2696/7. Telex: 47591 BARCTX G.
Contact: Competition Director.
Activities: Motor racing, hill climbs, sprints organised at most British tracks.

British Motor Racing Marshals Club, c/o Club Secretary Jack Ledgard, 51 Shenley Road, Bletchley, Milton Keynes, Bucks MK3 6HE. Tel: (0908) 72064.
Contact: As above.
Activities: Training, social events, provision of Emergency Service Teams at all circuits.

British Racing & Sports Car Club, Brands Hatch Circuit, Fawkham, Dartford, Kent DA3 8NH. Tel: (0474) 874445. Telex: 96172.
Contact: Competitions Director, John Nicol.
Activities: Championship, Formula Ford Festival & World Cup, and Motor Sports Show organisers.

Formula 2000 Association, 70 Nest Lane, Wellingborough, Northants NN8 4AX. Tel: (0933) 222903. Telex: 31612 OTSSG.
Contact: Val Adaway.
Activities: Club for all Formula Ford 2000 information.

Chassis manufacturers

The Crosslé Car Company Ltd, Rory's Wood, Old Holywood Road, Holywood, Co. Down, N. Ireland. Tel: (0232) 63332.
Contact: Colin Scott.
Manufacture of Crosslé racing cars.

Lola Cars Ltd, Glebe Road, St. Peter's Hill, Huntingdon, Cambs PE18 7DS. Tel: (0480) 51301. Telex: 32192.
Contact: Mike Blanchet.
Design, development, manufacture and sales of race-winning FF cars.

Reynard Racing Cars Ltd, Reynard Centre, Telford Road, Bicester, Oxon OX6 0UY. Tel: (0869) 244397/242615. Telex: 837497 SPAXSH G.
Contact: Rick Gorne.
Design, construction, development, sales, and innovation in Formulae Ford.

Royale Racing Ltd, 69 High Street, Riseley, Bedford. Tel: (023063) 581. Telex: 826311.
Contact: Alan Cornock.
Design, development, and sale of FF1600, 2000, and Sports 2000.

Sparton Engineering Ltd, 'Oaks', Hare Lane, Blindley Heath, Lingfield, Surrey RH7 6JB. Tel: (0342) 834834.
Contact: Norman Pierce.
Racing car manufacturer, race hire, design and development work.

Ian Taylor Racing, Kiln Meadow, Oare, Hermitage, Newbury, Berks RG16 9SD. Tel: (0635) 200205/201528.
Contact: Ian Taylor.
Manufacture, development, sales and hire of Taylor Trainer FF car.

Van Diemen International Racing Services Ltd, Chalk Road, Snetterton, Norwich, Norfolk NR16 2JZ. Tel: (0953 87) 270.
Contact: Ralph Firman.
Manufacturer of race winning FF1600 and 2000 cars.

Zeus Racing Ltd, Unit 6G, Silverstone Circuit, Silverstone, Towcester, Northants NN12 8TN. Tel: (0327) 857988.
Contact: Peter Sneller.
Formula Ford car manufacturers. Fabricators in aluminium, steel, and GRP.

Engine tuners

Auriga Racing Engines Ltd, Brise Yard, Rowhill Road, Wilmington, Dartford, Kent DA2 7QQ. Tel: (0322) 60152.
Contact: Martin Spence.

Neil Brown Engineering, Brantons Bridge, Bourne Road, Spalding, Lincs PE11 1JN. Tel: (0775) 3052.
Contact: Neil Brown.

Minister Racing Engines, Unit F, Burnham Trading Estate, Burnham Road, Dartford, Kent DA1 5BW. Tel: (0322) 28342.
Contact: David Minister.

Scholar Automotive Developments, Building No. 25, Martlesham Heath, Ipswich, Suffolk IP5 7GT. Tel: (0473) 622855.
Contact: Mr. Wardropper.
Suppliers and rebuilders of FF1600 and 2000 and other competition engines.

Swindon Racing Engines Ltd, Crampton Road, Greenbridge Estate, Swindon, Wilts SN3 3JJ. Tel: (0793) 31321.
Contact: John Dunn.
Engines precision built and tested, from Formula Ford to Formula One.

Racing car preparation & hire

ADA Engineering, 58/76 Willow Vale, Shepherds Bush, London W12 0P8. Tel: (01) 743 4477. Telex: 883762.
Contact: Chris Crawford.
Complete racing services: suspension setting, repairs, gearbox rebuilds, spares.

Andreason Racing, The Moorside, Winnall Trading Estate, Winchester, Hants SO23 7RX. Tel: (0962) 60755.
Contact: R. I. Andreason or L. J. Heighway.
General race preparation and spares supplier. Chevron Sports 2000 manufacturer.

British Racing Prospects (Silverstone) Ltd. Unit 23, Silverstone Circuit, Towcester, Northants NN12 8TL. Tel: (0327) 857310. Telex: 311164 SC BRDC.
Contact: Gerry Corbett.
Driver and sponsor orientated race hire in Formula Ford.

Rob Cresswell Racing Services, Warren Wood, Faygate, Sussex RH12 4SS. Tel: (029 383) 585.
Contact: Rob Cresswell or Dave Linksted.
FF1600 and 2000 car preparation and hire, and gearbox rebuilds.

The Hampshire Automobile Racing Team, G2 Ford Brook Estate, Marlborough Road, Pewsey, Wiltshire. Tel: (06726) 3329.
Contact: Richard Speakman or Michael Thorne.
FF1600 team and driver management, sponsor liaison and promotions service, sales and preparation team.

Ray Joyce Racing, Pitstop Garage, Willingham Road, Market Rasen, Lincs LN8 3DX. Tel: (0673) 842723.
Contact: Ray Joyce.

Agents for Delta Race Cars. FF1600 race hire and preparation team.

Madgwick Motorsport, Unit 6F, Silverstone Circuit, Towcester, Northants NN12 8TN. Tel: (0327) 857476/964. Telex: 311164 SCBRDC.
Contact: Robert Synge.
FF1600 and 2000 racing team, company promotions and entertainment days.

Nayler Road & Motorsport, Unit 6, Holly Hall Industrial Estate, Holly Hall Road, Dudley, West Midlands. Tel: (0384) 214152.
Contact: Richard Nayler.
Chassis, engine, and race preparation. Tiga race car agents, and for racewear.

Racefax International Race Hire & Preparation Services, Brise Yard, Rowhill Road, Wilmington, Kent. Tel: (0322) 60152 day or (0474) 63922 night.
Contact: Mike Baker.
FF1600 and 2000 race hire and preparation.

Racing Preparations (Cambridge), Stretham Station Road, Wilburton, Ely, Cambs CB6 3QD. Tel: (035389) 558.
Contact: Mark Dunham.
FF race hire and preparation specialists.

Rushen Green Racing, Snetterton Circuit, Norwich, Norfolk, NR16 2JU. Tel: (095387) 8152 or (0603) 54069.
Contact: Dennis Rushen or Robin Green.
FF1600 and 2000 preparation, hire, and management.

Ian Taylor Racing, Kiln Meadow, Oare, Hermitage, Newbury, Berks RG16 9SD. Tel: (0635) 200205/201528.
Contact: Ian Taylor.
Race hire and preparation of Taylor Trainer.

Promotion, PR, & paperwork services

Formula Services, 70 Nest Lane, Wellingborough, Northants NN8 4AX. Tel: (0933) 222903. Telex: 31612 OTSS G.
Contact: Val Adaway.
Complete paperwork service for racing drivers, covering all formulae.

Paul Davies Public Relations, Willow House, Mustill's Lane, Over, Cambridge CB4 5PW. Tel: (0954) 31199. Telex: 817340.
Contact: Paul Davies or Phillip Bingham.
Specialists in all areas of motoring and motor sports public relations.

Silverscreen (Fine Screen Prints), Power House, Low Friar Street, Newcastle-Upon-Tyne NE1 5UF. Tel: (0632) 324842. Telex: 53440.
Contact: Keith Wickham.
Manufacturers of promotional and publicity material, especially stickers, decals, clothing.

Speedsport Promotions Ltd, Anglia House, 78/84 High Street, Houghton Regis, Dunstable, Beds LU5 5BJ. Tel: (0582) 68141.
Contact: Mike O'Brien or Julia Govier.
Sponsorship consultancy, organisation of company promotional days and hospitality at circuits.

Team Schemes, 5 Stoneleigh Park Road, Ewell, Epsom, Surrey KT19 OQR. Tel: (01) 394 2228.
Contact: Nigel Smith.
Manufacturers of promotions material, such as T-shirts and stickers, specialising in motor sport.

Publications

Autosport, Haymarket Publishing Ltd, 38-42 Hampton Road, Teddington, Middx. Tel: (01) 977 8787. Telex: 8952440.
Contact: Assistant Editor, Marcus Pye.
Motor sports news magazine, published every Thursday, price 70p.

Campaign, Haymarket Publishing Ltd, 22 Lancaster Gate, London W2 3LY. Tel: (01) 402 4200. Telex: 8954052.
Contact: Editorial Assistant, Penny Sayer.
Trade journal of advertising and marketing, published every Friday, price 60p.

Motoring News, News Publications Ltd, Standard House, Bonhill Street, London EC2A 4DA. Tel: (01) 628 4741. Telex: 888602 MONEWS G.
Contact: National racing editor, Simon Arron.
Motor sports newspaper, published every Wednesday, price 30p.

Sponsorship News, Charterhouse Business Publications, 31A Rose Street, Wokingham, Berks RG11 1XS. Tel: (0734) 792066.
Contact: Editor/Publisher, Jonathan Gee.
The UK's only sponsorship magazine, monthly, £30 for annual subscription.

Schools

Peacock International Racing Drivers' Schools, South Street, Caerwys, Mold, Clwyd CH7 5AL. Tel: (0352) 720398.

Contact: Richard Peacock or Rosemary Crossle.
Racing drivers' schools at Aintree, Liverpool, and Kirkistown, N. Ireland.

Jim Russell International Racing Drivers' School, London Road, Downham Market, Norfolk PE38 ODF. Tel: (0366) 383397. Telex: 817459.
Contact: Managing Director, John Paine.
World famous racing drivers' school, at Snetterton, Norfolk. (Branches also in USA).

Silverstone Racing School Ltd, Unit 22, Silverstone Circuit, Silverstone, Towcester, Northants NN12 8TL. Tel: (0327) 857177. Telex: 311164 SC BRDC.
Contact: Mr. D. Smith.
Formula Ford and saloon tuition, including school races.

Ian Taylor Racing Drivers' School Ltd, Kiln Meadow, Oare, Hermitage, Newbury, Berks RG16 9SD. Tel: (0635) 200205/201528.
Contact: Ian Taylor.
Racing drivers' school run by British Sports 2000 frontrunner, at Thruxton.

Team Touraco International Racing Drivers' School, Northolme Industrial Estate, Louth, Lincs. Tel: (0507) 601726 (24 hrs), or Holland 070 522859.
Contact: Graeme Glew (UK) or Guy Csonka (Europe).
International Racing Drivers' school, and race preparation team.

Other useful addresses

Avon Tyres Ltd, Bath Road, Melksham, Wiltshire SN12 8AA. Tel: (0225) 703101. Telex: 44142.
Contact: Mr. E. Wood or Mr. R. K. Everson.
Producers and sellers of racing tyres.

T. L. Clowes Insurance Brokers Ltd, 6/8 Fenchurch Buildings, London EC3M 5HR. Tel: (01) 480 5371. Telex: 8956607 clowes.
Contact: Karen, Tim, or Joanna.
Insurance brokers for all business specialising in motor racing.

Dunlop Auto Racing Tyres, 15B Station Field Industrial Estate, Kidlington, Oxon OX5 1JD. Tel: (08675) 71991/2.
Contact: Steve Ball.
Producers and sellers of racing tyres, including Formula Ford.

Ferodo Limited, Chapel-en-le-Frith, Stockport, SK12 6JP. Tel: (0298) 812520. Telex: 667784.
Contact: Alan Campbell or Owen Sykes, Competitions Department.
Manufacturers and sellers of disc brake pads and brake linings.

Jaybrand Raceware, Highbury Street, Peterborough PE1 3BH. Tel: (0733) 68347. Telex: 32376.
Contact: Roger Hawkins.
Manufacturer of race and rally flameproof clothing and mechanics overalls. Helmet stockists.

Lucas Girling Ltd, Parts and Service Division, Birmingham Road, West Bromwich, West Midlands B71 4JR. Tel: 021-553-2969. Telex: 338801.
Contact: Sales Manager, Mr. G. Smith.
Brake and actuation technologists for cars, commecial vehicles, trains, racing cars.

Sabre Automotive Ltd, Reynard Centre, Telford Road, Bicester, Oxon OX6 0UY. Tel: (0869) 242615/244397. Telex: 837497 SPAXSH G.
Contact: Rick Gorne.
Motor racing fabrication and chassis repairs.